BIG BOOK OF
BRAIN GAMES

Andrews McMeel
Publishing®

Kansas City • Sydney • London

Andrews McMeel Publishing, LLC
an Andrews McMeel Universal company
1130 Walnut Street, Kansas City, Missouri 64106

www.andrewsmcmeel.com

All puzzles supplied under license from Puzzler Media Ltd.
www.puzzler.com

15 16 17 18 19 PAH 10 9 8 7 6 5 4 3 2

ISBN: 978-1-4494-6488-2

Made by:
The P. A. Hutchison Company
Address and location of production:
400 Penn Avenue, Mayfield, PA 18433 USA
2nd printing – 2/27/15

1 Quest

All the answers to the clues are four-letter words, and you have to enter them into the grid, starting from the outer squares. When you have done that, the innermost squares clockwise from number 9 will spell the name of a shape.

1 Posted a letter
2 Opposite of rich
3 Cab
4 Wild cat
5 Stingy, nasty
6 Bird's limb
7 Fishes' breathing organ
8 Flying toy

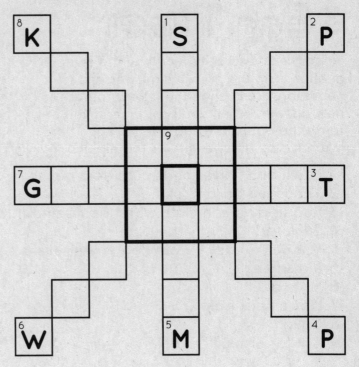

2 Cross Out

Each of the squares in this crossword grid contains two letters. Can you cross out one letter in each square so that the remaining letters spell out words in all rows and columns? We've crossed out the **S** in the top left-hand square to start you off.

S C	W	E	D	R
O R	H A	L N	I	Y H
E U	X V	L	M	A P
B A	Y	Y A	C	T
L M	R O		T	W
	U L	W M	G M	Y E

3 Egg Timer

To answer these clues, you have to remove a letter from the previous answer and (if necessary) rearrange the letters to get the new answer. When you pass clue 5, you have to do the opposite—add a letter each time. We have put in one answer to help you.

1 Lawn and flower beds outside a house
2 Thousand dollars (slang)
3 Repair a hole in cloth with needle and thread
4 Sprinted
5 ~~You can't teach __ old dog new tricks, old saying~~
6 Male adult
7 Lion's neck hair
8 Called
9 Ask for firmly

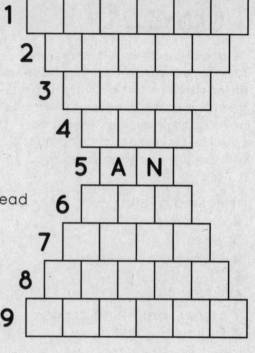

4 Splitz

The six-letter answers to these clues have been split into two in the jumbled heap of words. Can you solve the clues by putting the words back together? When the grid is complete, transfer the letters to the appropriate boxes in the lower grid to discover an Australian animal.

1 Car's shelter
2 Facial feature that blinks
3 T-shirt fabric
4 ~~Archer~~
5 House feature made of glass
6 Word a director shouts to start filming

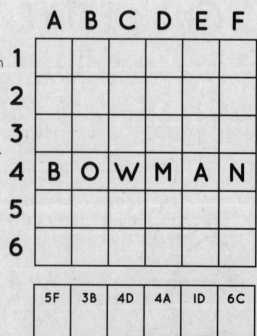

ACT   TON   ~~BOW~~   GAR   WIN   EYE

DOW   LID   AGE   ~~MAN~~   COT   ION

5 Figurework

Here's a kriss kross with a difference. This time it's figures instead of words.

2 figures
13
29
33
36
46
54
58
65
74
78
81
92

3 figures
177
199

214
275
348
489
490
513
597
690
736
865
996

4 figures
2528
3100
4215
5644

6308
7743
9219
9503

5 figures
42296
64765

7 figures
4029761

6 X-word

The answers to these clues are all five-letter words ending in **S**, the center letter. Write your answers in the grid starting from the outer squares, then rearrange the shaded letters to discover something nasty a bee can do.

1 Capital city of France
2 Sturdy footwear
3 Bird's arms
4 Baked ____, canned food

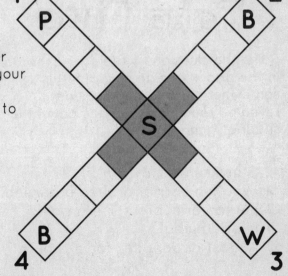

7 Change-a-letter

Solve the clues below, changing one letter of your answer at a time. When you get to clue 12, you'll find that its answer is also one letter different from the first answer, **RING**.

1 Finger jewelery
2 Part of an airplane
3 Drink made from grapes
4 Furniture wood
5 Stack, heap
6 Light-colored
7 Piece of window glass
8 Stab of hunger
9 Sound of an explosion
10 Group of musicians
11 South African currency
12 Orange peel

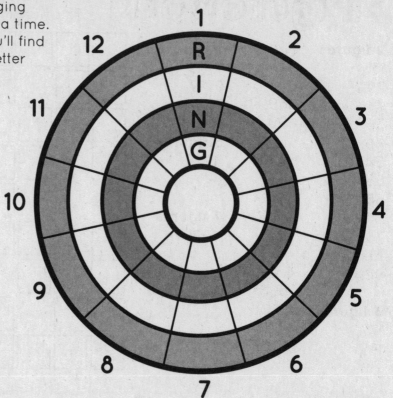

8 Take Five

Solve the clues and write your answers in the grid. If you do so correctly, somewhere nice to go to will be revealed reading diagonally down the shaded squares.

1 Sturdy shoes
2 Wooden barrier around a garden
3 Python or cobra, for example
4 Midday meal
5 August or January, for example

9 Bull's-eye

For each of the targets, find two letters that, when placed in the center, will form three six-letter words.

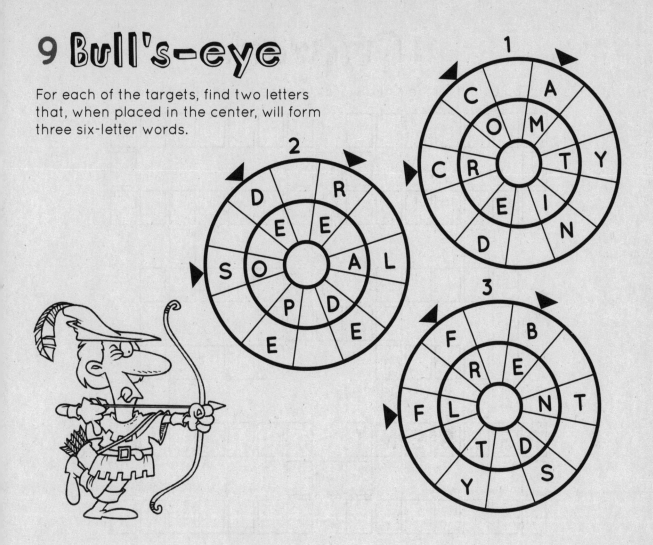

10 Leftovers

Cross out any letter that appears more than once in line A. The remaining letters will form an answer to line B.

A KOOKABURRAS
B Public transport

11 Gridwork

Can you fit all the listed words into the symmetrical grid?

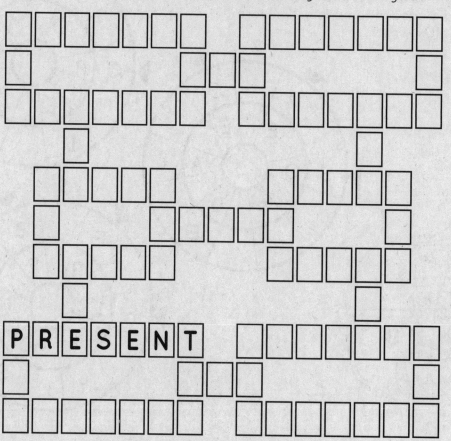

3 letters		**5 letters**	**7 letters**
AIM	OWE	AHEAD	CONQUER
ASH	OWN	LOONY	EVENING
COS	PIE	MINCE	FIANCEE
DAY	ROW	OPERA	INVITED
DOE	SAT	PRISM	KNOBBLY
ELK	TUG		NETWORK
FEN	URN		PRESENT
ICE	YAM		SWALLOW
INK			
LAP			

12 Clockwords

In this puzzle, there are two letters in place of each number on the clockface. To make a clockword, write down the letters that the hour hand points to, then the letters that the minute hand points to. For example, twenty-five to one would make the word **TIPS**. Now, using the clockface, work out the eight clockwords below, which are all associated with running.

1 Five to eight
2 Quarter past ten
3 Twenty-five to nine
4 Twenty past one
5 Five to five
6 Nine o'clock
7 Ten past five
8 Half past one

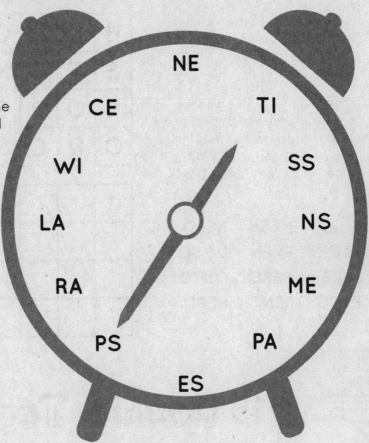

NE
CE   TI
WI   SS
LA   NS
RA   ME
PS   PA
ES

13 Word Ladder

Can you climb down the word ladder from **SNAP** to **SHOT**? Simply change one letter in SNAP for the answer to the first clue, then one letter in that answer for the answer to the second clue, and so on.

CLUES

1 Strike with a flat hand
2 Slide; skid
3 Large boat
4 Place to buy things

S	N	A	P
1			
2			
3			
4			
S	H	O	T

14 Magic Boxes

In a magic box, the words read the same across and down, just like this:

H	E	R	O
E	T	O	N
R	O	P	E
O	N	E	S

Have a go at making three more magic boxes using the words listed below, making sure that the word **HERO** appears once in each box.

SHED	MESH	HERO
SLUR	EVEN	DOSE
ELLE	HERO	ONTO
EROS	RENT	HERO

15 Double Trouble

For each row, both answers have four letters. The first answer finishes in the gray circle, while the second answer starts in the gray circle. When you've finished, the gray circles will spell out an adjective and the gray squares will spell out a different one.

1 Male children • Opposite of fast
2 Cab • Device for ironing clothes
3 Round throwing toy • Baby sheep
4 Soccer net • Adore
5 Simple • Twelve months

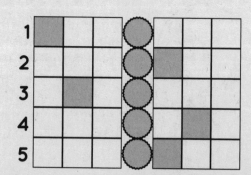

16 Trellis

Here's a kriss kross with a difference. All the words are four letters long, and they read diagonally downward to the right and to the left. The last letter of one word is the first of the next, and the circles show where the words start.

AFAR
GLOW
GOAT
HAIL
KILN
LAST
LESS
NAVY

NEST
PAIR
PEEL
RISK
ROOT
SONG
TOWN
TWIG

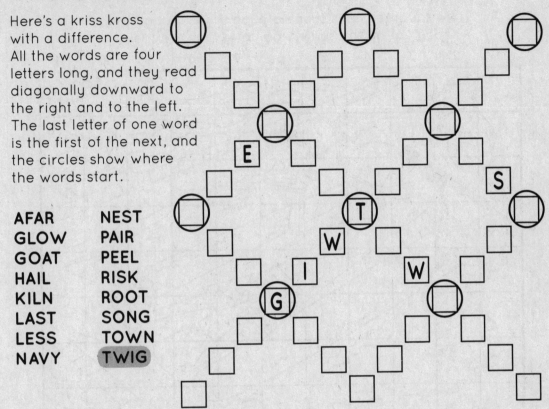

17 Name Game

Solve the clues and fill in the missing letters in the spaces provided. Then take the missing letters, in order, to discover what the Invisible Man calls his mom and dad.

1 Way in   EN _ _ ANCE
2 Mother's mother   GR _ _ DMOTHER
3 Building for sick people   HO _ _ ITAL
4 Begins   ST _ _ TS
5 Middle   C _ _ TER
6 Diver's garment   WE _ _ UIT

18 Square Eyes

Two squares in this scene are identical, though they
may not be the same way up. Which are they?

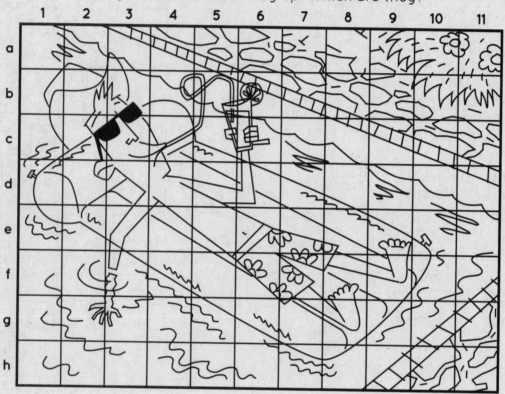

19 Spot the Sum

In each of these boxes, there are two numbers that can be added together
to make one of the other numbers. For example, 2, 3, and 5 in a box
would be the correct numbers, because 2 + 3 = 5. Circle the correct three
numbers in each box.

17   6   9   12
                    1
24 29 34 39

19   8   12   18
                    3
21 25 32 42

20 Pyramids

The number in each circle is the sum of the two below it, so in the first puzzle, the number shown in the third row down must be 8 because 3 + 5 = 8. Can you fill in all three pyramids?

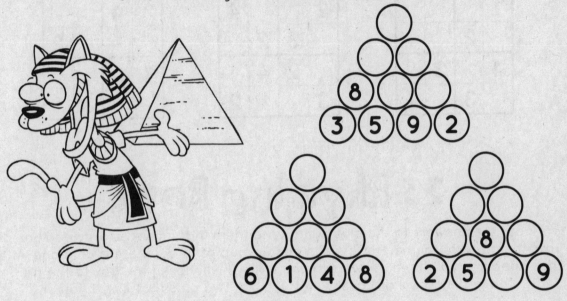

21 Elimination

Look at the categories and cross out all the words that belong to any of those categories. You can start by crossing out all the GIRLS' NAMES in the list. When you've crossed out the words from all four categories, there will be two words left. Put these words together, and what do you get?

CATEGORIES
Girls' names • Family members • Star signs • Hats

Beret	Capricorn	Libra	Mobile
Aunty	Cap	Mary	Turban
Phone	Jane	Sombrero	Scorpio
Aries	Brother	Susan	Catherine
Helen	Father	Mother	Uncle

22 Sudoku

Place numbers in the empty squares so that each row, each column, and each 2x2 block contains all the numbers from 1–4.

Grid 1:

1			
	2		
4		3	
	3		1

Grid 2:

2			4
	3	2	
	2	4	
3			2

Grid 3:

	4		
			2
1			
		3	

23 Rhyming Rows

Work out the answers to the clues and write them in the spaces provided. In each row, the answers rhyme. However, in each group of three, there is only one letter that appears in all three answers. If you write this letter in the box to the right of the grid, you will discover what you call two pigs that live together.

1 Animal's foot (3) 2 Look around a new area (7) 3 Without money (4)
4 Fib (3) 5 Farewell (7) 6 Organ of sight (3)
7 Horse's strap (4) 8 Ache (4) 9 Country road (4)
10 Pastry dish (3) 11 Snoop (3) 12 Thickness of wool (3)
13 Labyrinth (4) 14 Sunbeams (4) 15 Lay around (4)
16 Sledge (6) 17 Take part in a game (4) 18 Set the table (3)
19 Cutting tool (3) 20 Get a goal (5) 21 Noise made when asleep (5)

1		2		3		
4		5		6		
7		8		9		
10	PIE	11	PRY	12	PLY	P
13		14		15		
16		17		18		
19		20		21		

24 Shadow Play

Have a go at putting the fourteen pictures in order, starting with the shortest shadow and finishing with the longest.

25 Quest

All the answers to the clues are four-letter words. Enter them into the grid, starting from the outer squares. When you have done that, the innermost squares clockwise from number 9 will spell out something connected with school reading.

1 Money
2 Martial art
3 Ray of light
4 Elm or oak
5 Went by plane
6 Reflected sound
7 Twelve months
8 Bird's bill

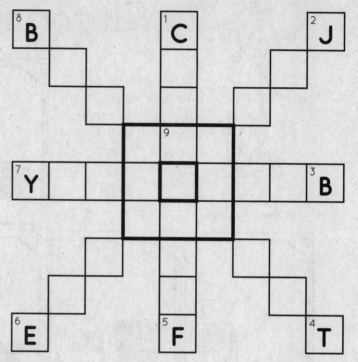

26 Cross Out

Each of the squares in this crossword grid contains two letters. Can you cross out one letter in each square so that the remaining letters spell out words in all rows and columns? We've crossed out the **B** in the top left-hand square to start you off.

B̶/S	T/A	V/I	E/U	M/R
L/U	C/I			A/P
D/E	W/N	D/E	E/H	O/D
E/I		E/P		I/W
C/P	H/I	L/O	L/T	O/Y

27 Egg Timer

To answer these clues, you have to remove a letter from the previous answer and (if necessary) rearrange the letters to get the new answer. When you pass clue 5, you have to do the opposite—add a letter each time. We have put in one answer to help you.

1 Female parent
2 Bart Simpson's dad
3 Place to live
4 ~~Gardening tool~~
5 The man
6 That woman
7 Rabbitlike animal
8 Vital body organ
9 Male parent

28 Splitz

The six-letter answers to these clues have been split into two in the jumbled heap of words below. Can you solve the clues by putting the words back together? When the grid is complete, transfer the letters to the appropriate boxes in the lower grid to reveal who swings through the jungle backward.

1 Food cupboard, larder
2 Sofa
3 Complete chaos
4 ~~Toothed fastener~~
5 Angler's bait
6 Mother's husband

GOT   TRY   ~~PER~~   HER   MAY   TEE

MAG   PAN   SET   ~~ZIP~~   FAT   HEM

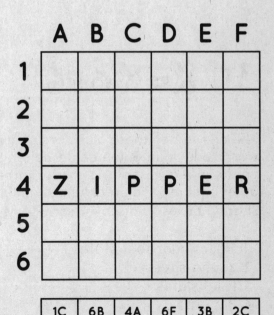

29 Figurework

Have a go at fitting all the listed numbers into the grid.

2 figures	4 figures	7 figures
10	2013	3463102
22	4028	5140976
35	4360	
67	6423	**9 figures**
84	6771	205583389
93	7417	796331214
	8532	

3 figures	9137
216	
400	**5 figures**
782	42806
793	99871
868	

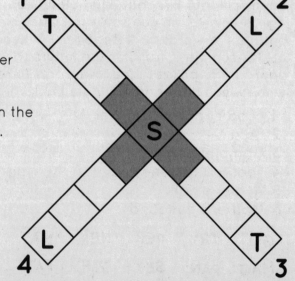

30 X-word

The answers to these clues are all five-letter words ending in **S**, the center letter. Write your answers in the grid starting from the outer squares, then rearrange the letters in the shaded boxes to discover something tasty.

1 Second largest state
2 Young sheep
3 Roof slates
4 Big cats

31 Change-a-letter

Solve the clues below, changing one letter of your answer at a time. When you get to clue 12, you'll find that its answer is also one letter different from the first answer, **BANK**.

1 Money business building
2 Bed above or below another
3 Dollar (slang)
4 Bird that waddles and quacks
5 Dip a cookie in a hot drink
6 Submerged underwater
7 Kitchen basin
8 Close one eye quickly
9 Strong breeze
10 Magician's stick
11 Beach grains
12 Musical group

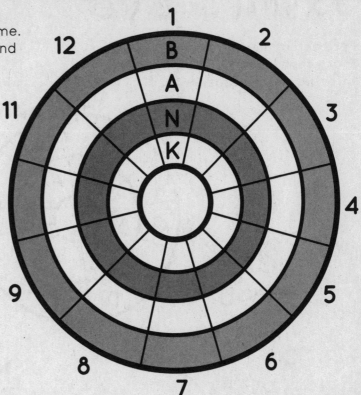

32 Sudoku

Place numbers in the empty squares so that each row, each column, and each 3x3 block contains all the numbers from 1–9.

1	5				4	7		
		2		1				8
4	3	8	7		9			
8					2			
	6	7				5	3	
			5					2
		9		1	3	7	5	
7				5		1		
	3	2					4	9

33 Bull's-eye

For each of the targets, find two letters that, when placed in the center, will form three six-letter words.

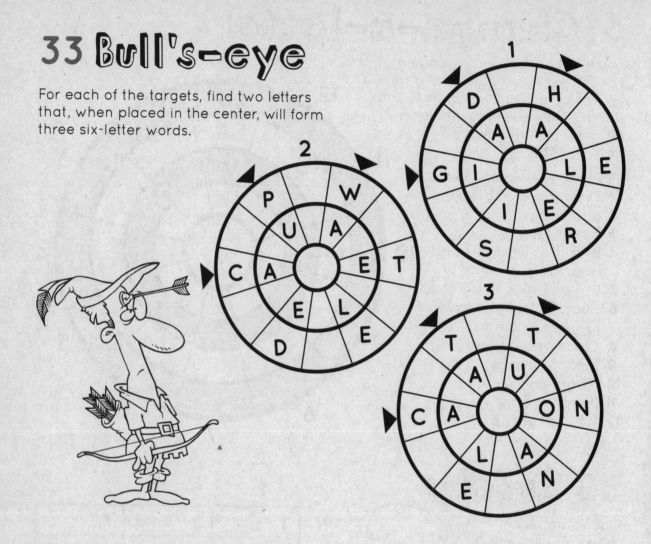

34 Leftovers

Cross out any letter that appears more than once in line A. The remaining letters will form an answer to line B.

A HAPPY HOLIDAYS
B Firm, stable

35 Gridwork

Can you fit all the listed words into the symmetrical grid?

| C | A | M | E | O |

3 letters
APT
BEG
COB
DIP
ELK
ERA

FRY
HAS
KIT
MIX
NEO
NOD
ODD

OUR
SKI
TIP
VAN

5 letters
ACORN
BIPED
CAMEO
FLUSH
INGOT
NAMED

PRONG
SHARK
TEMPO
THROB
VIXEN
YEARS

BONUS Wheely Words

If you place a letter in the center circle, you can combine it with the jumbled letters in each section to make six numbers. What letter should be placed in the center to complete the six numbers?

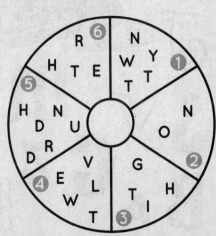

36 Alphabet Soup

To discover what the girl's name is, work out which four letters appear three times in the picture. Rearrange them to reveal her name. Some of the letters of the alphabet are missing. When rearranged, those letters will reveal the name of her horse.

37 Clockwords

In this puzzle, there are two letters in place of each number on the clockface. To make a clockword, write down the letters that the hour hand points to, then the letters that the minute hand points to. For example, five to six would make the word **STIR**. Now, using the clockface, work out the eight clockwords.

1 Twenty to two
2 Quarter past seven
3 Twenty-five past six
4 Five past four
5 Seven o'clock
6 Half past nine
7 Five past two
8 Half past ten

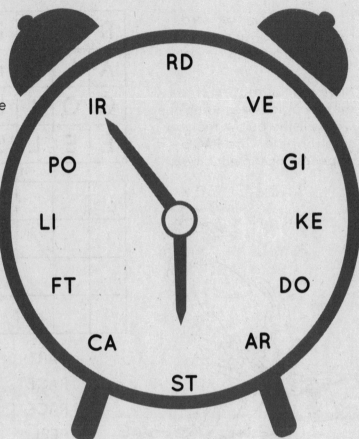

38 Break Out

An instrument has gone missing from the orchestra. If you cross out every letter in the grid that appears more than once, the remaining letters will reveal what type of instrument is missing.

P	F	C	A	I
C	I	V	B	L
U	A	C	I	P
P	B	V	T	E

39 Magic Boxes

In a magic box, the words read the same across and down, just like this:

Have a go at making three more magic boxes using the words listed below, making sure that the word **RACE** appears once in each box.

R	A	C	E
A	L	O	E
C	O	I	L
E	E	L	S

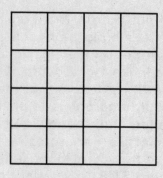

DART	TRAP	COLA
RACE	TREE	ALEC
RACE	ACHE	SCAR
PEEL	AFAR	RACE

40 Word Ladder

Can you climb down the word ladder from **MESS** to **NEAT**? Just change one letter in MESS for the answer to the first clue, then one letter in that word for the answer to the second clue, and so on.

CLUES

1 Loch ____ Monster, legendary creature
2 Bird's home
3 Little exam
4 Better than all the others
5 Drummer's rhythm

M	E	S	S
1			
2			
4			
4			
5			
N	E	A	T

41 Trellis

Here's a kriss kross with a difference. All the words are four letters long, and they read diagonally downward to the right and to the left. The last letter of one word is the first of the next, and the circles show where the words start.

BOSS
CHIP
CLUB
DISC
DUEL
EPIC
FIGS
FOAM

LIMB
LUCK
MATE
MIND
SPED
STEW
TEAM
WELL

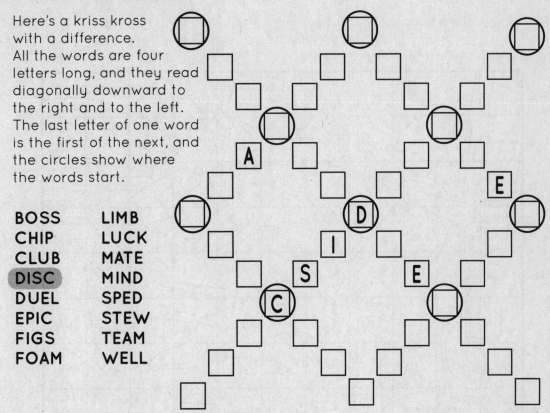

42 Name Game

Complete the answers to these clues, then take the missing letters, in order, to reveal what Luke Skywalker shaves with.

1 Royal home
2 Gift
3 Popular doll
4 Lettuce, cucumber, tomatoes, etc.
5 Set of portable steps

PA _ _ C E
PRE _ _ N T
BA _ _ I E
SA _ _ D
LAD _ _ R

43 Square Eyes

Two squares in this scene are identical, though they may not be the same way up. Which are they?

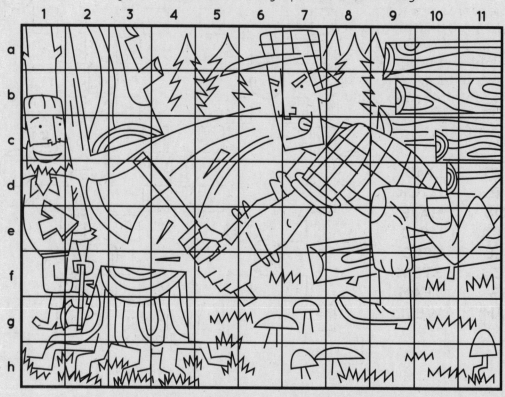

44 Spot the Sum

In each of these boxes, there are two numbers that can be added together to make one of the other numbers. For example, 2, 3, and 5 in a box would be the correct numbers, because 2 + 3 = 5. Circle the correct three numbers in each box.

1   17   26   40   6
9   22   44   29

12   29   34   8   3
14   28   27   19

45 Pyramids

The number in each circle is the sum of the two below it, so in the first puzzle, the number shown in the third row down must be 11 because 2 + 9 = 11. Can you fill in all three pyramids?

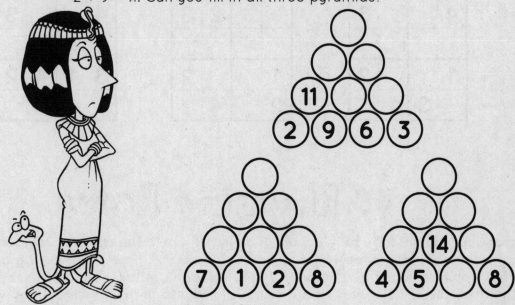

46 Elimination

Look at the categories and cross out all the words that belong to any of those categories. You can start by crossing out all the BOYS' NAMES in the list. When you've crossed out the words from all four categories, there will be two words left. Put these words together, and what do you get?

CATEGORIES
Boys' names • Months • Sports • Parts of the body

Leg	Golf	Basketball	Forty
January	Arm	John	Knee
Winks	Michael	Elbow	Hockey
Football	March	George	Tim
Peter	November	April	December

47 Sudoku

Place numbers in the empty squares so that each row, each column, and each 2x2 block contains all the numbers from 1–4.

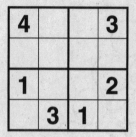

4			3
1			2
	3	1	

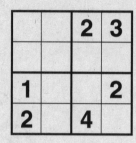

		2	3
1			2
2		4	

4			3
3	1	4	2

48 Rhyming Rows

Work out the answers to the clues and write them in the spaces provided. In each row, the answers rhyme. However, in each group of three, there is only one letter that appears in all three answers. If you write this letter in the box to the right of the grid, you will discover what the buffalo said to her child when they went their separate ways in the morning.

1 Shout of disapproval (3)   **2** Sky color (4)   **3** Exhaled air (4)

4 Tall (4)   **5** Fib (3)   **6** Pastry dish (3)

7 Looked at (3)   **8** Painful (4)   **9** Sports result (5)

10 Foot digit (3)   **11** Use oars (3)   **12** Cut grass (3)

13 ___ on the cob, vegetable (4)   **14** Chess piece (4)   **15** Baby deer (4)

1	BOO	2	BLUE	3	BLEW	B
4		5		6		
7		8		9		
10		11		12		
13		14		15		

49 Out of Order

Can you arrange these flags in order from the least filled-in to the full one?

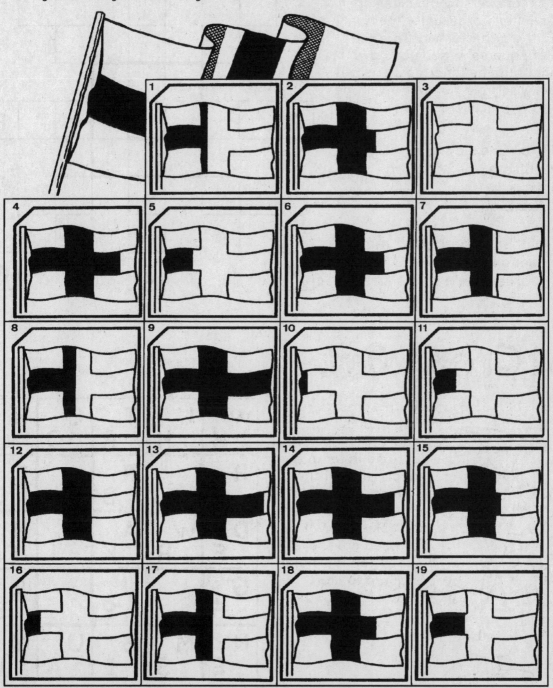

50 Quest

All the answers to the clues are four-letter words. Enter them into the grid, starting from the outer squares. When you have done that, the innermost squares clockwise from number 9 will spell out a mythical creature.

1 Husband's partner
2 Noise made by a lion
3 Naked
4 Get bigger
5 Nil
6 Dinner or breakfast, maybe
7 Young cow
8 Workers on a ship

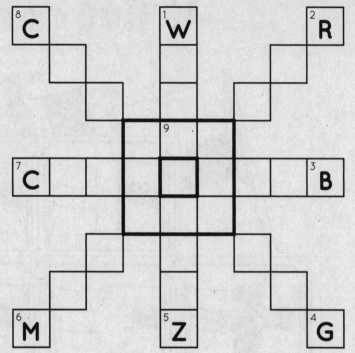

51 Cross Out

Each of the squares in this crossword grid contains two letters. Can you cross out one letter in each square so that the remaining letters spell out words in all rows and columns? We've crossed out the **W** in the top left-hand square to start you off.

W H	U H	T	C R	H O	P
R E		R B		O		C O
D F	W R	A K	O I	N		N I
G F		J P			L E
N E	M S	S E	U A	Y L	

52 Egg Timer

To answer these clues, you have to remove a letter from the previous answer and (if necessary) rearrange the letters to get the new answer. When you pass clue 5, you have to do the opposite—add a letter each time. We have put in one answer to help you.

1 Fitness, freedom from illness
2 ~~Moorlands~~
3 Warmth
4 Have a meal
5 Film alien
6 Mesh for catching fish
7 Lodger's payment
8 Go in
9 Middle

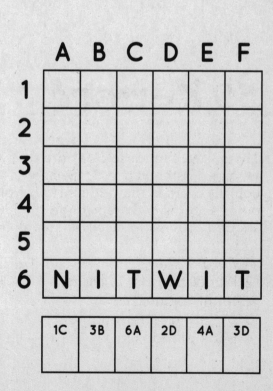

Row 2: H E A T H

53 Splitz

The six-letter answers to these clues have been split into two in the jumbled heap of words below. Can you solve the clues by putting the words back together? When the grid is complete, transfer the letters to the appropriate boxes in the lower grid to reveal what kind of tree provides the best food.

1 Say or do again
2 Sofa
3 Grand ____, major tourist attraction
4 Gone bad
5 Bright shiny metal
6 ~~Silly fool~~

A B C D E F

Row 6: N I T W I T

EAT   YON   ~~NIT~~   PER   REP   CAN
TEN   SET   TEE   ~~WIT~~   COP   ROT

1C	3B	6A	2D	4A	3D

54 Figurework

Have a go at fitting all the listed numbers into the grid.

2 figures	3 figures
19	134
23	471
36	612
42	637
48	744
51	801
61	
74	**4 figures**
80	2007
82	3412
93	4457
96	5169
	6223

	5 figures		7 figures
7034	33202	68613	2763531
7391	51147	91748	6013247
8885			

Grid contains: **8 0 1**

55 X-word

The answers to these clues are all five-letter words ending in **S**, the center letter. Write your answers in the grid starting from the outer squares, then rearrange the letters in the shaded squares to discover something sweet.

1 *Lord of the ____*, film
2 Planet and Ms. Williams, tennis player
3 ____ truly, letter ending
4 Book of maps

56 Change-a-letter

Solve the clues below, changing one letter of your answer at a time. When you get to clue 12, you'll find that its answer is also one letter different from the first answer, **PANG**.

1 Stab of hunger
2 Group of criminals
3 Warbled, trilled
4 Disappeared underwater
5 Army vehicle
6 Chore
7 Facial disguise
8 Creamed potato
9 Notes and coins
10 Group of actors
11 Time gone
12 Gasp

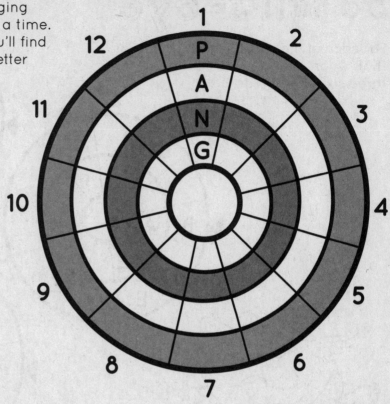

57 Sudoku

Place numbers in the empty squares so that each row, each column, and each 3x3 block contains all the numbers from 1–9.

					2			
2		6		3		4		
5			1	7	6		8	3
	7	2		6	9			
4		3				6		2
			2	5		7	3	
7	2		6	4	1			8
	1			2		9		4
		7						

58 Bull's-eye

For each of the targets, find two letters that, when placed in the center, will form three six-letter words.

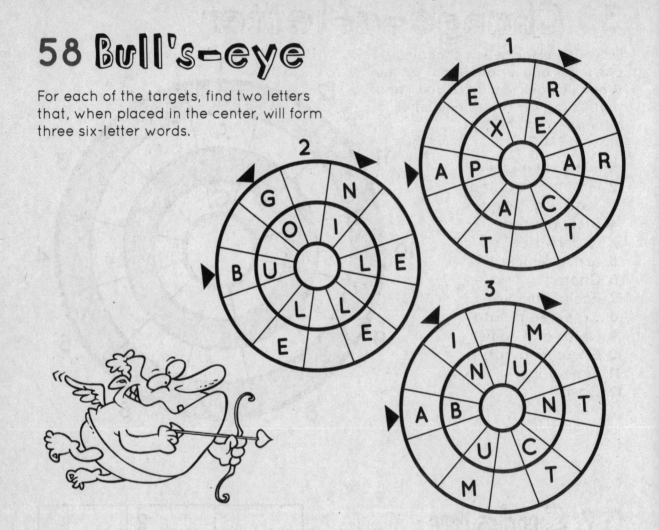

59 Break Out

A wild animal has escaped from the zoo. If you cross out every letter in the grid that appears more than once and rearrange the remaining letters, you'll find out what type of animal is on the loose.

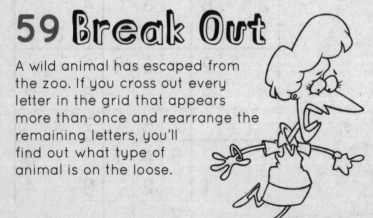

Q	E	U	G	A	P
F	Z	O	Y	W	S
T	H	Q	C	J	R
K	P	I	E	S	K
J	Y	D	F	G	T
L	W	O	C	H	U

60 Alphabet Soup

To discover what this man is called, work out which four letters of the alphabet are missing from the letter jumble. When rearranged, they will spell out his name. And to find out what he does for a living, rearrange the five letters that appear three times in the letter jumble.

61 Clockwords

In this puzzle, there are two letters in place of each number on the clockface. To make a clockword, write down the letters that the hour hand points to, then the letters that the minute hand points to. For example, half past two would spell **ROAD**. Using the clock and the times given, can you find five more clockwords?

1 Quarter to twelve
2 Five to five
3 Twenty past one
4 Twenty-five to three
5 Twenty to ten

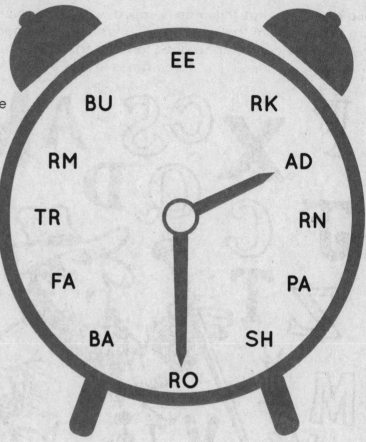

62 Six Down

Write the answers to the clues downward in the columns. The gray squares will spell out a word.

CLUES

1 Place to buy things
2 Two times two
3 Knobbly part of the leg
4 Leaf of a book
5 Croaking water creature
6 Objects that unlock doors

	1	2	3	4	5	6

63 Magic Boxes

In a magic box, the words read the same across and down, just like this:

A	N	T	S
N	O	A	H
T	A	X	I
S	H	I	P

Have a go at making three more magic boxes using the words listed below, making sure that the word **SHIP** appears once in each box.

MASK	SHIP	PEAR
KILO	KEPT	SHIP
HIDE	ASKS	ACHE
SPOT	IDEA	SHIP

64 Letter Pyramid

Each answer includes all the letters of the answer before it, plus one new letter. Finally, add one letter to answer 4 and rearrange them to spell out a type of fish.

1 ____ long!, a way of saying good-bye
2 ____ Angeles, large city
3 Too, as well
4 Hairdresser's or beauty shop

The fish is a __ __ __ __ __ __ .

65 Trellis

Here's a kriss kross with a difference. All the words are four letters long, and they read diagonally downward to the right and to the left. The last letter of one word is the first of the next, and the circles show where the words start.

BELL   LAUD
BREW   MUSH
FANG   PING
GIST   PITH
GRAB   SHOW
HERB   TOIL
HISS   WAND
LATE   WASP

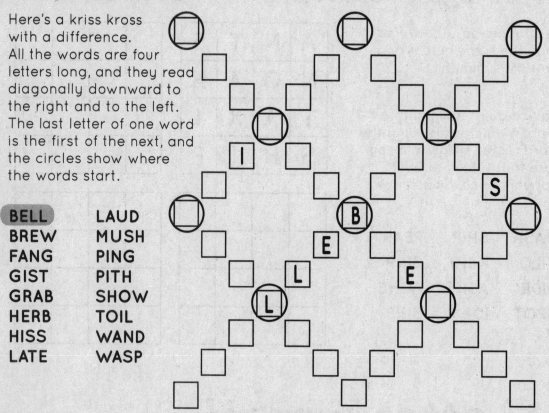

66 Name Game

Complete the answers to these clues, then take the missing letters, in order, to spell out an item of dishware.

1 Corridor   PAS __ __ G E
2 Type of bird   C __ __ K O O
3 Brave woman   H __ __ O I N E

67 Square Eyes

Two squares in this scene are identical, though they
may not be the same way up. Which are they?

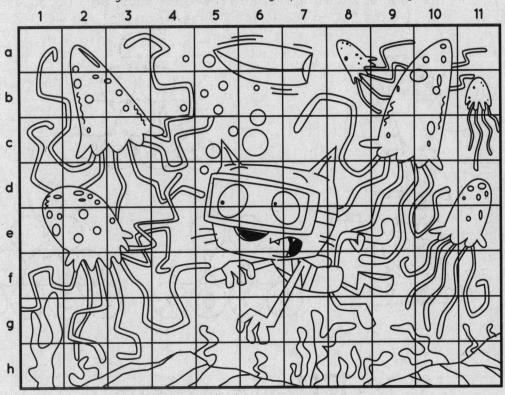

68 Spot the Sum

In each of these boxes, there are two numbers that can be added together
to make one of the other numbers. For example, 2, 3, and 5 in a box
would be the correct numbers, because 2 + 3 = 5. Circle the correct three
numbers in each box.

26 6 9 13 2
34 35 38 42

39 11 35 45 3
5 22 20 28

69 Pyramids

The number in each circle is the sum of the two below it, so in the first puzzle, the number shown in the third row down must be 5 because 2 + 3 = 5. Can you fill in all three pyramids?

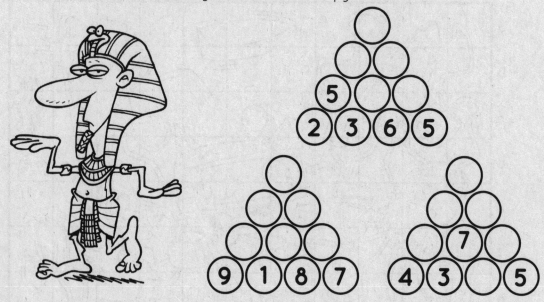

70 Elimination

Look at the categories and cross out all the words that belong to any of those categories. You can start by crossing out all the FLOWERS in the list. When you've crossed out the words from all four categories, there will be two words left. Put these words together, and what do you get?

CATEGORIES				
Words that can go in front of "baby" • Church features • Flowers • Words associated with piano				

Cry	Grand	Key	Hyacinth	Apse
Bolt	Altar	Thunder	Upright	Tuner
Nave	Crocus	Iris	Font	
Rose	War	Stool	Test tube	
Bush	Jelly	Aisle	Tulip	

71 Sudoku

Place numbers in the empty squares so that each row, each column, and each 2x2 block contains all the numbers from 1–4.

Grid 1

4	2	3	1
3			
			3
2	3	1	4

Grid 2

3		4	2
4			3
1			4
2	4		1

Grid 3

2			4
	4	2	
	2	1	
1			2

72 Rhyming Rows

Work out the answers to the clues and write them in the spaces provided. In each row, the answers rhyme. However, in each group of three, there is only one letter that appears in all three answers. If you write this letter in the box to the right of the grid, you will spell out a fun vehicle.

1 Icehouse (5)   2 Got bigger (4)   3 Paste for sticking things (4)
4 Black bird (4)   5 In the past (3)   6 Enemy (3)
7 Leg joint (4)   8 Travel on snow (3)   9 Lock opener (3)
10 Double ___, instrument (4)   11 Item of luggage (4)   12 Front of the head (4)
13 Make a mistake (3)   14 Cat's sound (4)   15 Mix with a spoon (4)
16 Two times four (5)   17 Packing box (5)   18 Hang about (4)

1		2		3		
4		5		6		
7		8		9		
10		11		12		
13	ERR	14	PURR	15	STIR	R
16		17		18		

73 Out of Order

Can you put these feathers in the correct order going from number 2, which is all white, to number 11, which is all black?

74 Quest

All the answers to the clues are four-letter words. Enter them into the grid, starting from the outer squares. When you have done that, the innermost squares clockwise from number 9 will spell out some fun transport.

1 Writing tools
2 White powder for the body
3 Nil, nothing
4 Stringed toy
5 Opposite of first
6 Number of legs on a starfish
7 Twinkling feature of the night sky
8 Messenger birds in the Harry Potter books

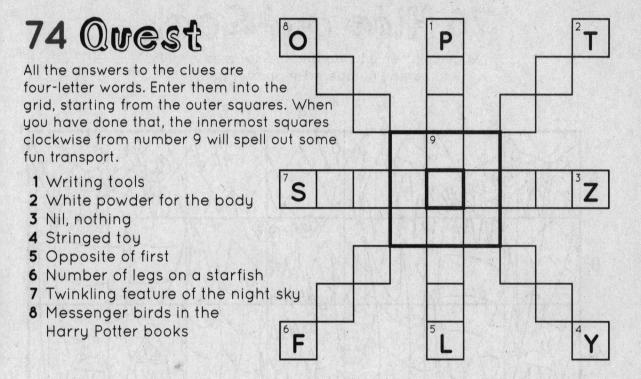

75 Cross Out

Each of the squares in this grid contains two letters. Can you cross out one letter in each square so that the remaining letters spell out words in all rows and columns? We've crossed out the **T** in the top left-hand square to start you off.

76 Hide and Seek

How quickly can you identify the squares in which
each of the numbered shapes appears?

77 Egg Timer

To answer these clues you have to remove a letter from the previous answer and (if necessary) rearrange the letters to get the new answer. When you pass clue 5, you have to do the opposite—add a letter each time. We have put in one answer to help you.

1 Cookery instructions
2 Cost
3 Ready to eat (of fruit)
4 Pastry dish
5 Games lesson (initials)
6 Round green vegetable
7 Superhero's cloak
8 Location, area
9 Type of fish

| 1 | R | E | C | I | P | E |

78 Splitz

The six-letter answers to these clues have been split into two in the jumbled heap of words below. Can you solve the clues by putting the words back together? When the grid is complete, transfer the letters to the appropriate boxes in the lower grid to spell out the name of Homer Simpson's friend.

1 Horse-like creature with long ears
2 Baby's footwear
3 Container for strawberries
4 Type of spice
5 Black and white bird
6 Road surface

MAC MAG BOO MEG PUN NET
TAR DON PIE TEE NUT KEY

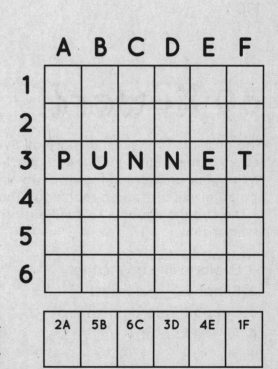

	A	B	C	D	E	F
1						
2						
3	P	U	N	N	E	T
4						
5						
6						

2A	5B	6C	3D	4E	1F

79 Figurework

Have a go at fitting all the listed numbers into the grid.

2 figures
16   56
27   65
35   73
36   82
42   88
50   89

3 figures
116
300
394
541
837
962

4 figures
1904
2141

3396
4800
5205
5356
8847
9153

5 figures
16007
32759

7 figures
1035447
2495037
7013361
7958812

80 X-word

The answers to these clues are all five-letter words ending in **T**, the center letter. Write your answers in the grid starting from the outer squares, then rearrange the letters in the shaded squares to spell out an area in the garden.

1 Explode like a volcano
2 Banana ____, dessert
3 Sound made by a sheep
4 Airline captain

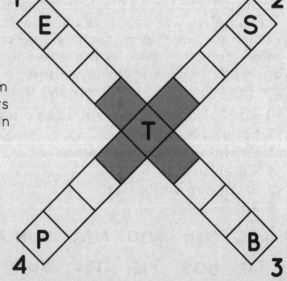

81 Change-a-letter

Solve the clues below, changing one letter of your answer at a time. When you get to clue 12, you'll find that its answer is also one letter different from the first answer, **WIDE**.

1 ~~Broad~~
2 Walk through water
3 Sea feature
4 Rouse from sleep
5 Cook in the oven
6 Sponge or angel food, for example
7 Item of luggage
8 Notes and coins
9 Creamed potatoes
10 Remove dirt
11 Desire for something, expressed when blowing out birthday candles
12 Clever, like an owl

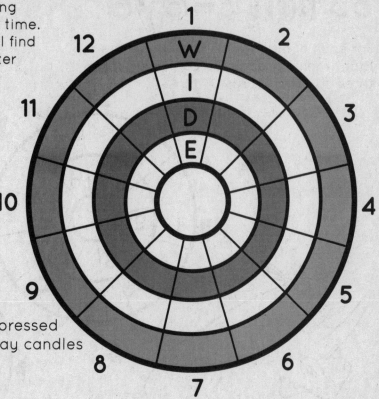

82 Sudoku ?

Place numbers in the empty squares so that each row, each column, and each 3x3 block contains all the numbers from 1–9.

			9	2	6			7
8	4	5			9			3
				4		1		
	9		1	2				
4		2				1		5
			4	3		8		
	8		4					
1			5			8	7	4
5				7	1	2		

83 Bull's-eye

For each of the targets, find two letters that, when placed in the center, will form three six-letter words.

84 Break Out

If you cross out any letter that appears more than once in the grid, the remaining letters will spell out a tasty snack.

S	B	Q	L	A
B	N	B	D	U
W	T	V	M	L
Q	L	M	I	V
U	C	T	Q	H

85 Alphabet Soup

To find out where Jim is going on vacation, work out which six letters are missing from the jumbled letters. Rearrange them to spell out the name of a country. The letters that appear more than twice can be rearranged to reveal where Sarah is going.

86 Trellis

Here's a kriss kross with a difference. All the words are four letters long, and they read diagonally downward to the right and to the left. The last letter of one word is the first of the next, and the circles show where the words start.

CHUG   OGRE
DODO   OINK
GOAT   PEER
GOSH   PING
HELM   READ
HERO   RICH
MINK   STAR
MOSS   TRAM

87 Name Game

Complete the answers to these clues, then take the missing letters in order to spell out the name of a mountain.

1 Red salad fruit   T O _ _ T O
2 Crispy coating on fish   B A _ _ E R
3 Sound system   S T _ _ E O
4 Teacher's workplace   S C _ _ O L
5 Big wasp   H O _ _ E T

88 Quest

All the answers to the clues are four-letter words. Enter them into the grid, starting from the outer squares. When you have done that, the innermost squares clockwise from number 9 will spell out a type of racing circuit.

1 Manager, person in charge
2 Leap, bound
3 Country road
4 Bird of peace
5 Where your fingers are found
6 Melt, defrost
7 Tiny bloodsucking insect
8 Color that is a mixture of black and white

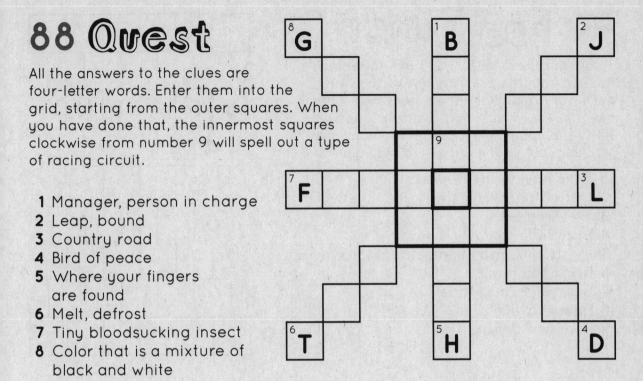

89 Cross Out

Each of the squares in this crossword grid contains two letters. Can you cross out one letter in each square, so that the remaining letters spell out words in all rows and columns? We've crossed out the **S** in the top left-hand square to start you off.

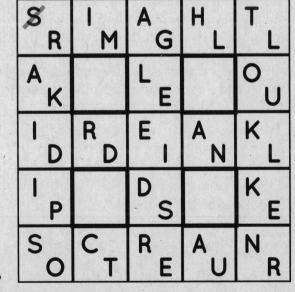

90 Egg Timer

To answer these clues, you have to remove a letter from the previous answer and (if necessary) rearrange the letters to get the new answer. When you pass clue 5, you have to do the opposite—add a letter each time. We have put in one answer to help you.

1 Bold, having the nerve
2 Outlet for used water
3 ~~Wet weather~~
4 Sprinted
5 ____ apple a day keeps the doctor away
6 Drink container
7 Scottish family, tribe
8 Spear, javelin
9 Removes dirt

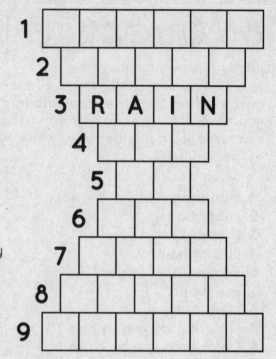

91 Splitz

The answers to these clues have been split into two in the jumbled heap of words below. Can you solve the clues and put them back together again in your answers? If you complete the grid correctly, you will be able to transfer the coded letters to the lower grid to spell out a type of nonsense word.

1 Headwear for hot weather
2 Small round disc on a shirt cuff
3 Wheel____, garden equipment
4 Male feline
5 ~~Hero, not the baddie~~
6 Told a lie

BUT HAT ~~DIE~~ CAT SUN FIB

ROW BAR TOM ~~GOO~~ TON BED

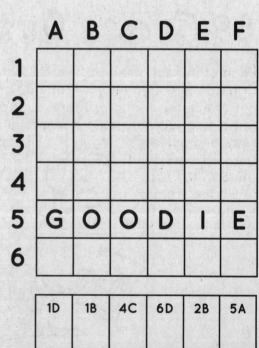

92 Figurework

Here's a kriss kross with a difference.
This time it's figures instead of words.

2 figures

18	69
33	74
35	80
42	86
54	91

3 figures

117	598
205	641
311	774
443	806
500	992

4 figures

1197

1672

1814
2289
3499
4932
5453
6326
7395
8541
8864
9180

9 figures

141044288
274517986

93 X-word

The answers to these four clues are all
five-letter words ending in the letter **E**.
Write your answers in the grid starting
from the outer squares, then rearrange the
shaded letters to spell out a type of dried fruit.

1 Church steeple
2 Pebble
3 Vine fruit
4 Sport or concert location

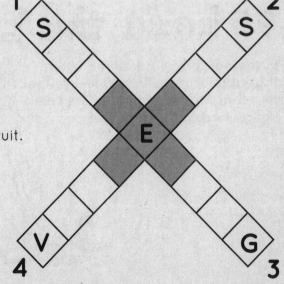

94 Change-a-letter

Solve the clues below, changing one letter of your answer at a time. When you get to clue 12, you'll find that its answer is also one letter different from the first answer, **DART**.

1 ~~Small arrow~~
2 Homer Simpson's son
3 Tree-trunk covering
4 Public gardens
5 Fill a suitcase
6 Choose
7 Hit with the foot
8 ____ Jagger, Rolling Stones singer
9 Small rodents
10 Game cubes
11 ____ straits, in big trouble
12 Filth, grime

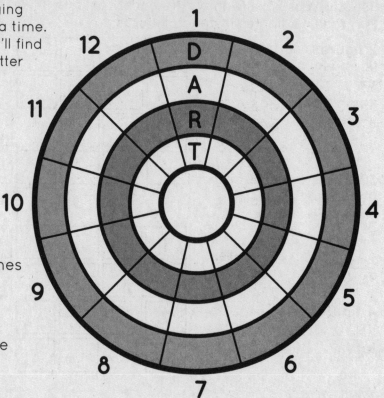

95 Lose the Letters

In the box, cross out all the letters that appear more than once. You will find that the remaining letters spell out a word that means wet.

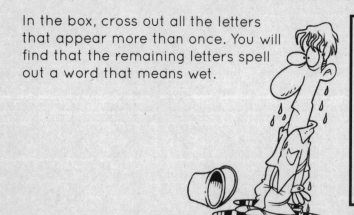

P S T U O
L A R F N
U K N P L
T E R F D

96 Bull's-eye

For each of the targets, find two letters that, when placed in the center, will form three six-letter words.

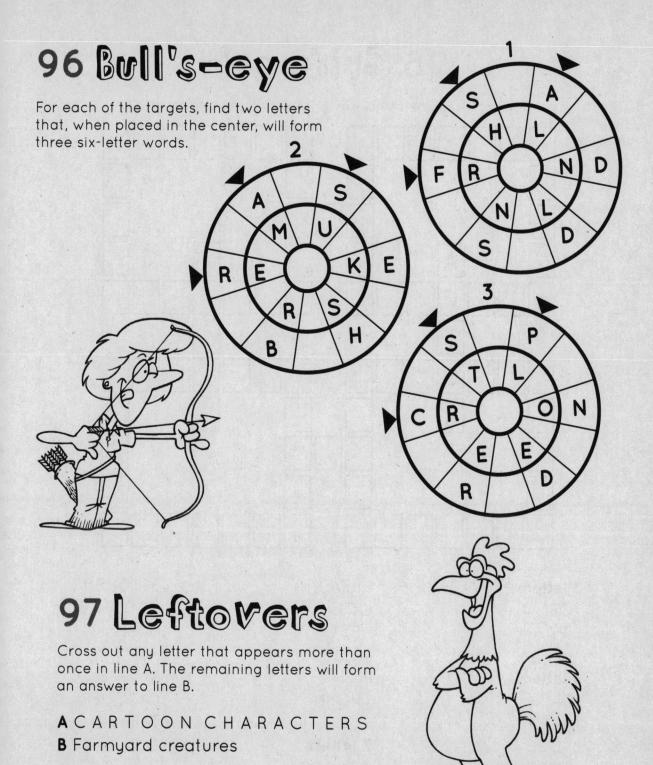

97 Leftovers

Cross out any letter that appears more than once in line A. The remaining letters will form an answer to line B.

A CARTOON CHARACTERS
B Farmyard creatures

98 Gridwork

Can you fit all the listed words into the symmetrical grid?

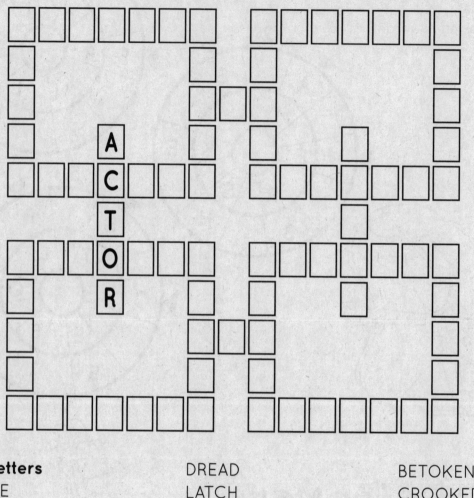

3 letters
TOE
OPT

5 letters
ABACK
ACTOR
BADGE
CHEST

DREAD
LATCH
NETTY
PILOT
RIGHT
THORN

7 letters
APRICOT

BETOKEN
CROOKED
EAGERLY
HABITAT
KITCHEN
LACQUER
TABLOID

99 Pick-Me-Up

Can you decide in what order
you would pick up the twelve
paintbrushes if you could only
take the top one each time?

100 Matchblocks

Can you put each block from group A in front of a different block from group B
to make eight four-letter words? For instance, MU and LE can be put together to
form MULE. Now see if you can match up the rest. Watch out, though—although
some group A blocks can match up with more than one block from group B, there
is only one way of using up all the blocks.

Group A

MU	SO	LE	BI	FA	BA	FO	PL

Group B

LE	AF	CE	RK	OP	AP	LL	OD

A	B		A	B		A	B
MU	LE						

101 Magic Boxes

In a magic box, the words read the same across and down, just like this:

I	R	I	S
R	E	D	O
I	D	E	A
S	O	A	P

Have a go at making three more magic boxes using the words listed below, making sure that the word **SOAP** appears once in each box.

SOAP	VAST	SPED
ONCE	SOAP	PEST
KATE	AHOY	SOAP
ACTS	TYPE	ASKS

102 Break Out

Another animal has escaped from the zoo. If you cross out every letter in the grid that appears more than once and rearrange the remaining letters, you'll find out what type of animal is on the loose.

M	A	S	B	O	C
F	D	V	J	P	G
X	N	H	Z	I	P
L	C	A	K	L	X
S	G	I	V	E	J
B	Y	Z	H	F	M

103 Trellis

Here's a kriss kross with a difference. All the words are four letters long, and they read diagonally downward to the right and to the left. The last letter of one word is the first of the next, and the circles show where the words start.

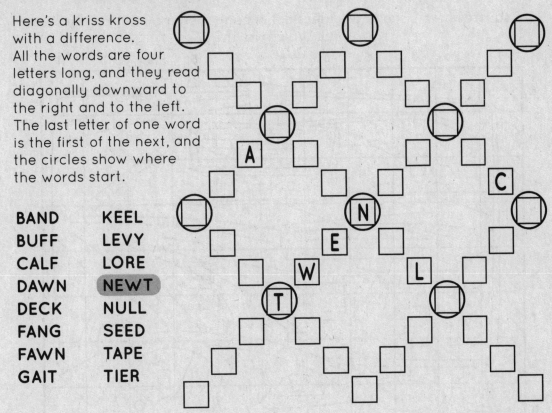

BAND	KEEL
BUFF	LEVY
CALF	LORE
DAWN	NEWT
DECK	NULL
FANG	SEED
FAWN	TAPE
GAIT	TIER

104 Name Game

Complete the answers to these clues, then take the missing letters, in order, to spell out an item of dishware.

1 Corridor   P A S _ _ G E

2 Type of bird   C _ _ K O O

3 Brave woman   H _ _ O I N E

105 Square Eyes

Two squares in this scene are identical, though they may not be the same way up. Which are they?

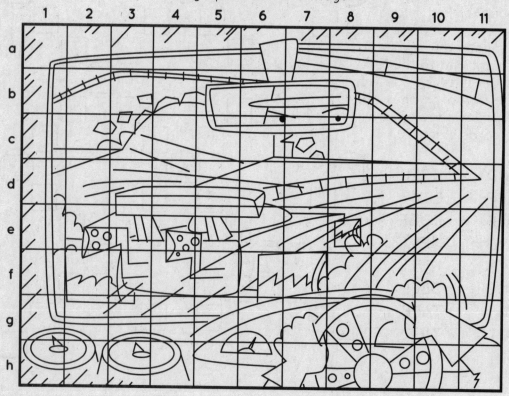

106 Spot the Sum

In each of these boxes, there are two numbers that can be added together to make one of the other numbers. For example, 2, 3, and 5 in a box would be the correct numbers, because 2 + 3 = 5. Circle the correct three numbers in each box.

9 21 37 3
27
36 7 19 32

13 24 45 40
8
20 2 23 31

107 Pyramids

The number in each circle is the sum of the two below it, so in the first puzzle, the number shown in the third row down must be 7 because 5 + 2 = 7. Can you fill in all three pyramids?

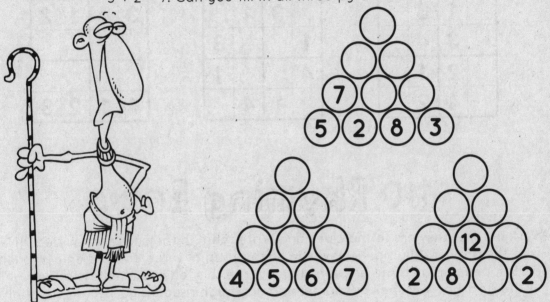

108 Elimination

Look at the categories and cross out all the words that belong to any of those categories. You can start by crossing out all the VEGETABLES in the list. When you've crossed out the words from all four categories, there will be two words left. Put these words together, and what do you get?

CATEGORIES
Fruits • Vegetables • Kitchen utensils • Big cats

Banana	Tiger	Carrot	Lettuce
Onion	Fork	Orange	Spatula
Spoon	Potato	Puma	Food
Lion	Apple	Strawberry	Pear
Processor	Knife	Cheetah	Cucumber

109 Sudoku

Place numbers in the empty squares so that each row, each column, and each 2x2 block contains all the numbers from 1–4.

Grid 1:

1	3		
3	4		
2	1		
4	2		

Grid 2:

	3	1	
1			3
4			1
	1	4	

Grid 3:

3	4	1	2
4	1	2	3

110 Rhyming Rows

Work out the answers to the clues and write them in the spaces provided. In each row, the answers rhyme. However, in each group of three, there is only one letter that appears in all three answers. If you write this letter in the box to the right of the grid, you will spell out something you might need if you go on vacation.

1 Seven of these in a week (4) **2** Sleds pulled by reindeer (7) **3** Lift up (5)

4 Pool stick (3) **5** Sky color (4) **6** Large African antelope (3)

7 Glistened, gleamed (5) **8** Elton ___, singer (4) **9** Long-necked, elegant bird (4)

10 Bashful, timid (3) **11** Opposite of low (4) **12** Deep breath (4)

13 Tool for chopping wood (3) **14** Candle substance (3) **15** Groups of wolves (5)

16 Words on a school badge (5) **17** Numbers game (5) **18** Rich cake (6)

1		2		3		
4		5		6		
7		8		9		
10		11		12		
13		14		15		
16	MOTTO	17	LOTTO	18	GATEAU	T

111 Out of Order

Can you put these number sevens in the correct order going from number 17, which is all white, to number 9, which is all black?

112 Quest

All the answers to the clues are four-letter words. Enter them into the grid, starting from the outer squares. When you have done that, the innermost squares clockwise from number 9 will spell out a type of crook.

1 Throw a pancake
2 Part of a school year
3 List of meals in a restaurant
4 Not short
5 Slimy garden pest
6 Back of the foot
7 Very strong wind
8 Grizzly or polar, for example

113 Cross Out

Each of the squares in this crossword grid contains two letters. Can you cross out one letter in each square, so that the remaining letters spell out words in all rows and columns? We've crossed out the **Q** in the top left-hand square to start you off.

114 Egg Timer

To answer these clues, you have to remove a letter from the previous answer and (if necessary) rearrange the letters to get the new answer. When you pass clue 5, you have to do the opposite—add a letter each time. We have put in one answer to help you.

1 *Treasure ___*, classic novel
2 Garden creature with a shell
3 Fingertip covering
4 ~~___ Fleming, James Bond writer~~
5 *Wind ___ the Willows*, story
6 Tailor's metal fastener
7 Measure of milk
8 Colored art liquid
9 A way of recording something

(Grid:)
1
2
3
4 I A N
5
6
7
8
9

115 Splitz

The six-letter answers to these clues have been split into two and placed in the jumbled heap below. Can you solve the clues by putting the words back together? When the grid is complete, transfer the letters to the appropriate boxes in the lower grid to spell out a tasty fruit.

1 On dry land
2 Floor covering
3 Late-night meal
4 Larder
5 Inspector ___, cartoon character
6 ~~Container for strawberries~~

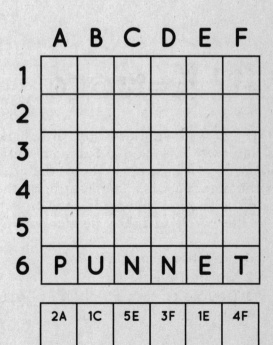

A B C D E F

1
2
3
4
5
6 P U N N E T

| 2A | 1C | 5E | 3F | 1E | 4F |

SUP   PAN   ~~PUN~~   GAD   PET   CAR

ORE   GET   PER   ~~NET~~   TRY   ASH

116 Figurework

Have a go at fitting all the listed numbers into the grid.

2 figures

25	64
36	71
42	77
55	86

6701
6872
7098
8565
9948

3 figures

126	672
261	688
360	704
408	799
443	948

5 figures

14058
38424
62573

7 figures

2038610
5547329
6128024
9001751

4 figures

1308
1923
2214

(Grid with the digits 6, 8, 8 pre-filled)

117 X-word

The answers to these clues are all five-letter words ending in **S**, the center letter. Write your answers in the grid starting from the outer squares, then rearrange the letters in the shaded squares to spell out what sort of writer wrote Casper's life story.

1 Breathes a sound of relief
2 Garden pests
3 Double or ____, gambling phrase
4 Spanish for good-bye

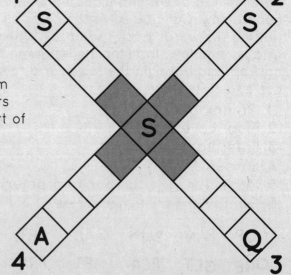

118 Change-a-letter

Solve the clues below, changing one letter of your answer at a time. When you get to clue 12, you'll find that its answer is also one letter different from the first answer, **FEEL**.

1 Touch
2 Gas
3 Opposite of empty
4 Male cow
5 Bouncy toy
6 Corridor
7 Small mountain
8 Tablet
9 Cash register
10 Opposite of short
11 Inform, relate
12 Toppled over

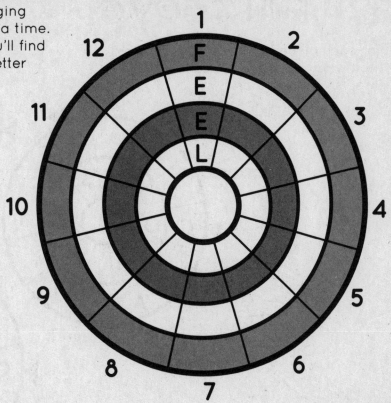

119 Sudoku

Place numbers in the empty squares so that each row, each column, and each 3x3 block contains all the numbers from 1–9.

	9	7					4	
2				5		8	1	
5			4	8				
			8			3		4
4	2		5		3		6	1
3		9			1			
				1	5			6
	3	2		9				8
	1					4	2	

120 Bull's-eye

For each of the targets, find two letters that, when placed in the center, will form three six-letter words.

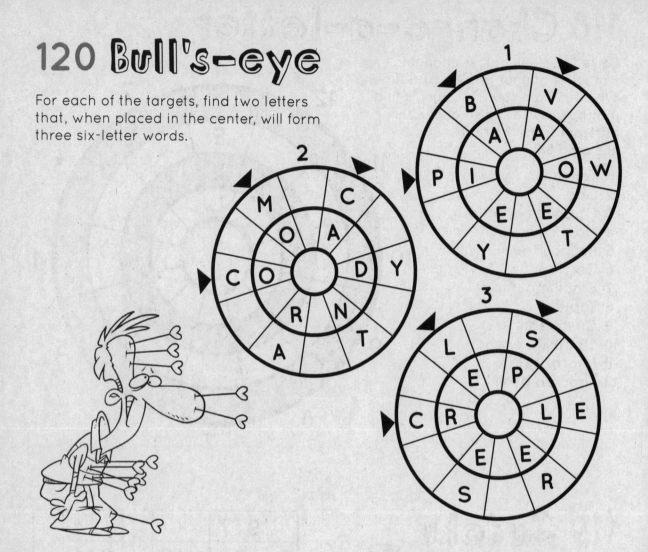

121 Leftovers

Cross out any letter that appears more than once in line A. The remaining letters will form an answer to line B.

A ALICE IN WONDERLAND
B Black bird

122 Gridwork

Can you fit all the listed words into the symmetrical grid?

3 letters
AIL
WOW

5 letters
ASTER
BEACH
BOWER
CHOIR
CLIFF
COAST
DOWSE
DRAFT
FRAIL
GECKO
GRAND
HILLS
NIGHT
OCHRE
PLEAD
PYLON
ROSES
TRAIL

(In grid: B E A C H)

123 Add Up

The number in each circle is the total of the two below it. You can see that the white number must be 38 because 22 + 16 = 38. Can you work out all the numbers in the circles?

124 Alphabet Soup

To discover this man's name, work out which five letters of the alphabet are missing. When rearranged, these letters will spell out his name. Then decide which six letters appear three times to discover what flavor soup he is eating.

125 It's All Over

The word **OVER** can come before all the listed words.
Can you fit them all into the kriss kross grid?

3 letters
ALL
ARM
EAT

4 letters
DONE
FLOW
HEAD
RIDE
TAKE
TIME
TONE

5 letters
BOARD
DRESS
GROWN
NIGHT
THROW

6 letters
COOKED
SHADOW
WEIGHT

7 letters
CROWDED
EXCITED

8 letters
ESTIMATE
SPENDING

9 letters
CONFIDENT

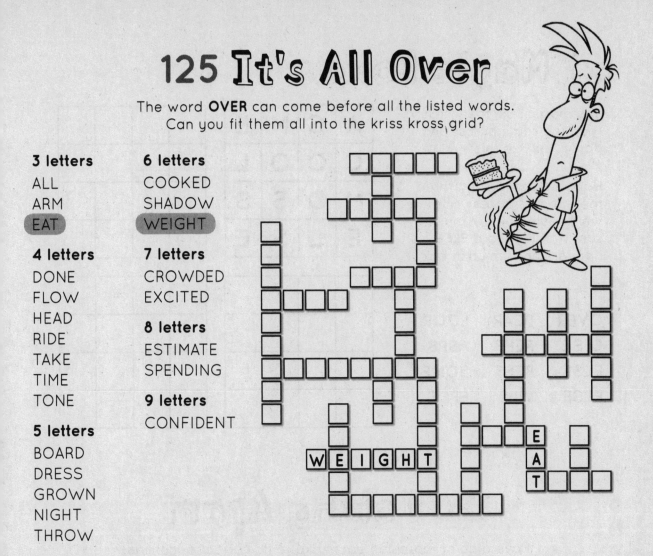

126 Mixed Fruits

This puzzle is all about types of fruit. See if you can
find all the listed words in this mini word search.

APRICOT
CHERRY
FIG
LEMON

MANGO
MELON
NECTARINE
OLIVE

ORANGE
PEAR
PLUM

N	Y	T	L	G	N	M
O	R	O	E	I	E	A
L	R	C	M	F	C	N
E	E	I	O	K	T	G
E	H	R	N	A	A	O
M	Y	C	P	B	Z	R	P
Y	R	R	A	E	P	I	L
O	L	I	V	E	N	U
O	R	A	N	G	E	M

127 Magic Boxes

In a magic box, the words read the same across and down, just like this:

A	C	M	E
C	O	O	L
M	O	S	S
E	L	S	E

Have a go at making three more magic boxes using the words listed below, making sure that the word **ELSE** appears once in each box.

OVER	DEAR	LOOP
ELSE	REEF	ASPS
ELSE	REST	SOME
ELSE	VILE	EPEE

128 Joking Apart

Have a go at matching each joke to its correct punchline.

1 Why did the chewing gum cross the road?
2 What do you get if you cross an ocean with a crook?
3 How can you get out of a locked music room?
4 What do you call a Stone Age cowboy?
5 What is round and red and goes up and down?
6 Why did the snake walk out of his math lesson?

A Play the piano till you find the right key
B Flint Eastwood
C Because he'd adder-nough
D Because it was stuck to the chicken's foot
E A tomato in an elevator
F A crime wave

129 Trellis

Here's a kriss kross with a difference. All the words are four letters long, and they read diagonally downward to the right and to the left. The last letter of one word is the first of the next, and the circles show where the words start.

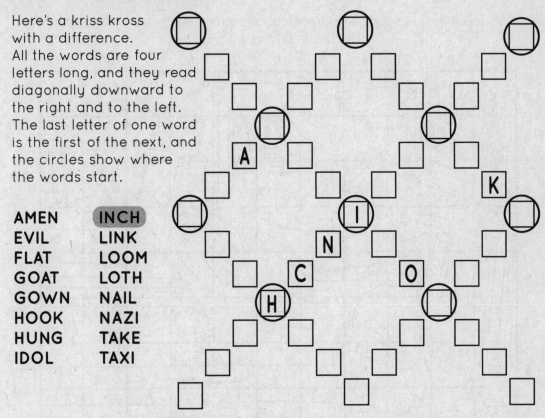

AMEN   INCH
EVIL   LINK
FLAT   LOOM
GOAT   LOTH
GOWN   NAIL
HOOK   NAZI
HUNG   TAKE
IDOL   TAXI

130 Name Game

Complete the answers to these clues, then take the missing letters in order to spell out an item of furniture.

1 Gulp   S _ _ L L O W

2 Lawn and flowerbeds   G A _ _ E N

3 The day after today   T O M O R _ _ W

4 Statue of ___, U.S. landmark   L I _ _ R T Y

131 Square Eyes

Two squares in this scene are identical, though they may not be the same way up. Which are they?

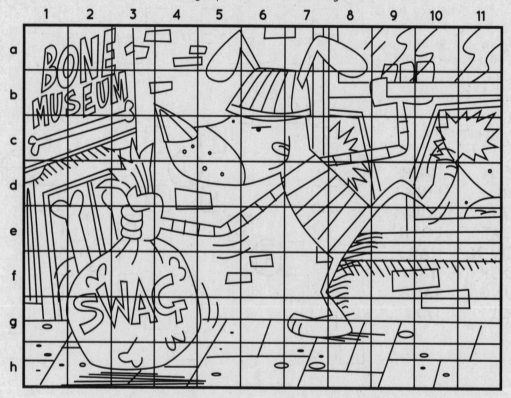

132 Spot the Sum

In each of these boxes, there are two numbers that can be added together to make one of the other numbers. For example, 2, 3, and 5 in a box would be the correct numbers because 2 + 3 = 5. Circle the correct three numbers in each box.

5 23 17 11 33
21 14 29 31

31 16 28 5 24
41 37 9 34

133 Pyramids

The number in each circle is the sum of the two below it, so in the first puzzle, the number shown in the third row down must be 15 because 9 + 6 = 15. Can you fill in all three pyramids?

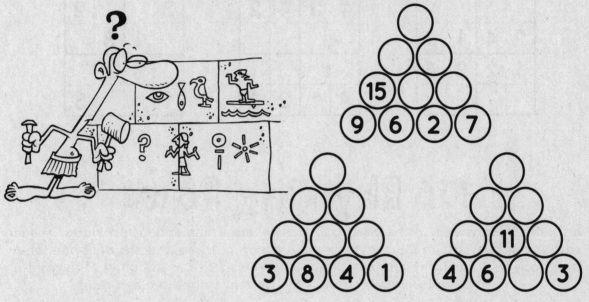

134 Elimination

Look at the categories and cross out all the words that belong to any of those categories. You can start by crossing out all the DRINKS in the list. When you've crossed out the words from all four categories, there will be two words left. Put these words together, and what do you get?

CATEGORIES
Simpsons characters • Musical instruments • Fish • Drinks

Homer	Salmon	Trumpet	Lisa
Piano	Milk	Cod	Drum
Herring	Pool	Bart	Pike
Water	Marge	Tea	Coffee
Guitar	Juice	Swimming	Maggie

135 Sudoku

Place numbers in the empty squares so that each row, each column, and each 2x2 block contains all the numbers from 1-4.

2	4	1	3
1	2	3	4

1	3	4	2
4	1	2	3

3			2
	1	3	
	3	2	
1			3

136 Rhyming Rows

Work out the answers to the clues and write them in the spaces provided. In each row, the answers rhyme. However, in each group of three, there is only one letter that appears in all three answers. If you write this letter in the box to the right of the grid, you will spell out a noble person from the olden days.

1 Lock opener (3) **2** Leg joint (4) **3** Travel on snow (3)

4 Elton ____, singer (4) **5** Disappeared (4) **6** Adult cygnet (4)

7 Chooses (5) **8** Three times two (3) **9** Mend, repair (3)

10 Sticky paste (4) **11** Via (7) **12** Got bigger (4)

13 Bashful (3) **14** Upper leg (5) **15** Opposite of low (4)

16 Not false (4) **17** Number in a duo (3) **18** Casserole (4)

1		2		3		
4		5		6		
7		8		9		
10	GLUE	11	THROUGH	12	GREW	G
13		14		15		
16		17		18		

137 Out of Order

Starting at 12:20 (picture 11) can you put the clocks in order as they tick forward? You should finish at 11:14 (picture 10). Careful . . . it's quite tricky, but you can take your time. Ha ha.

138 Quest

All the answers to the clues are four-letter words. Enter them into the grid, starting from the outer squares. When you have done that, the innermost squares clockwise from number 9 will spell out something sporty.

1 Small branch
2 Reflection of sound
3 Molten matter from a volcano
4 Tug, drag
5 Assist
6 Martial art
7 Touch lips romantically
8 Watercourse around a castle

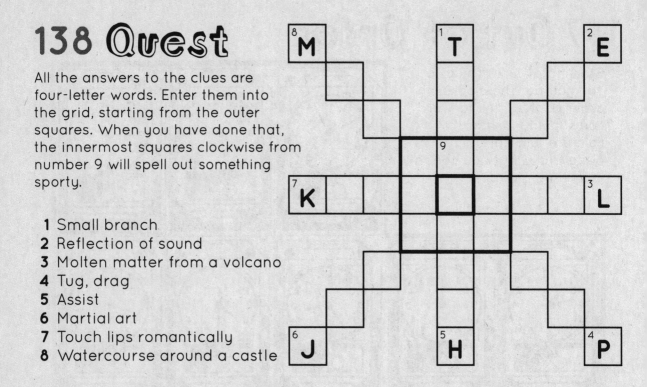

139 Cross Out

Each of the squares in this crossword grid contains two letters. Can you cross out one letter in each square so that the remaining letters spell out words in all rows and columns? We've crossed out the **T** in the top left-hand square to start you off.

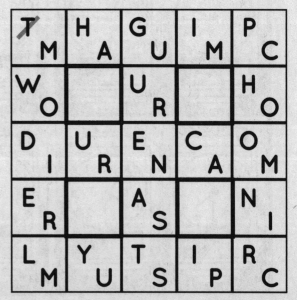

140 Egg Timer

To answer these clues, you have to remove a letter from the previous answer and (if necessary) rearrange the letters to get the new answer. When you pass clue 5, you have to do the opposite—add a letter each time. We have put in one answer to help you.

1 Climbing apparatus
2 Great fear
3 Have the nerve
4 Crimson color
5 Emergency Room initials
6 The woman
7 Brave man
8 Beach, coastline
9 Animals that cowboys ride

141 Splitz

The six-letter answers to these clues have been split into two and placed in the jumbled heap below. Can you solve the clues by putting the words back together? When the grid is complete, transfer the letters to the appropriate boxes in the lower grid to spell out a family member.

1 Pane of glass in a house
2 Mend
3 Picnic basket
4 Drive crazy
5 City in Switzerland
6 Say no

EVA   GEN   MAD   PER   REF   USE
WIN   AIR   REP   DEN   HAM   DOW

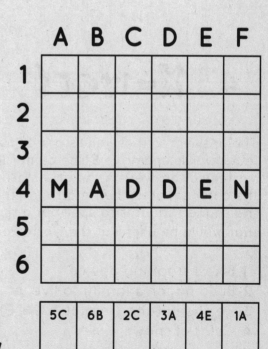

142 Figurework

Have a go at fitting all the listed numbers into the grid.

2 figures	3 figures (col 2)	4 figures (col 3)
351	2009	
13	392	3105
15	417	7830
27	425	
42	458	**5 figures**
56	544	11057
60	629	42208
82	703	74316
98	863	80264
	981	

2 figures
13
15
27
42
56
60
82
98

351
392
417
425
458
544
629
703
863
981

2009
3105
7830

5 figures
11057
42208
74316
80264

3 figures
176
216

4 figures
1092

7 figures
5021529
7489653

| | | | | | | | | **4** | **5** | **8** |

143 X-word

The answers to these clues are all five-letter words ending in **E**, the center letter. Write your answers in the grid starting from the outer squares, then rearrange the letters in the shaded squares to spell out a type of fish that would be useful at the North Pole.

1 Bike's stopping device
2 Building for a family to live in
3 Seaweed (anagram of A GALE)
4 Color of snow

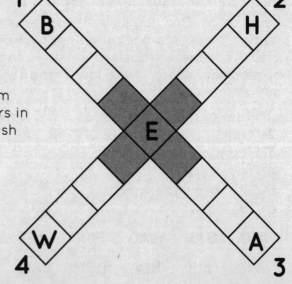

144 Change-a-letter

Solve the clues below, changing one letter of your answer at a time. When you get to clue 12, you'll find that its answer is also one letter different from the first answer, **FOAL**.

1 ~~Young horse~~
2 Solid black fuel
3 Warm winter garment
4 Seagoing vessel
5 Sturdy footwear
6 Underground part of a plant
7 Sound made by an owl
8 Captain ____, Peter Pan's enemy
9 Something to read
10 Make a hot meal
11 Chilly, cold
12 Daft person

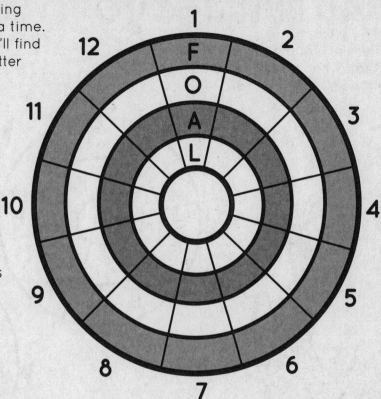

145 Sudoku

Place numbers in the empty squares so that each row, each column, and each 3x3 block contains all the numbers from 1–9.

					8			
				1		2	9	4
3	5	9			4			7
		6		3	5	7		2
		1	3			6	4	
5			4	2	1		8	
9				5		4	6	1
4	2	5		1				
				8				

146 Bull's-eye

For each of the targets, find two letters that, when placed in the center, will form three six-letter words.

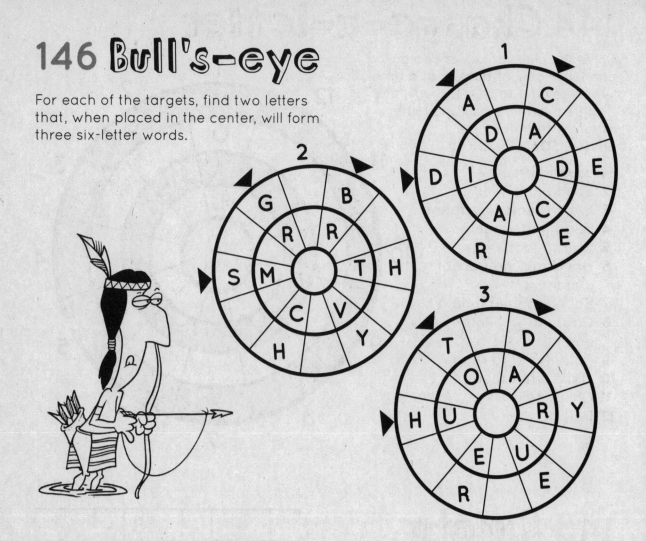

147 Break Out

Another animal has escaped from the zoo. If you cross out every letter in the grid that appears more than once and rearrange the remaining letters, you'll find out what type of animal is on the loose.

Q	T	I	O	B	U
P	W	S	Y	R	F
D	O	Z	G	H	K
H	Y	J	Q	I	D
F	T	U	E	J	W
J	A	S	G	K	P

148 Alphabet Soup

There are four letters that appear three times below. Work out which ones they are and rearrange them to discover what the little girl is called. Then rearrange the five letters of the alphabet that are missing to discover the name of her cute kitten.

149 Tune In

See if you can fit all these musical instruments into the grid.

4 letters
GONG
HARP
TUBA

5 letters
BANJO
FLUTE
ORGAN
PIANO
SITAR

6 letters
GUITAR
VIOLIN

7 letters
CYMBALS
OCARINA
TRUMPET

8 letters
BAGPIPES
MANDOLIN

9 letters
ACCORDION
HARMONICA
SAXOPHONE
XYLOPHONE

12 letters
GLOCKENSPIEL

G
U
I
T
A
R

150 At the Beach

This puzzle is all about the beach. See if you can find all the listed words in this mini word search.

CLIFF
DUNES
LIMPETS
PEBBLES

POOLS
ROCKS
SEAWEED
SHELLS

SHINGLE
TIDE
WAVES

U	F	D	E	P	S	S
L	F	D	O	E	E	K
T	I	O	R	B	V	C
T	L	M	V	B	A	O
S	C	L	P	L	W	R
S	E	A	W	E	E	D
D	U	N	E	S	T	S
E	L	G	N	I	H	S
S	H	E	L	L	S	X

151 Magic Boxes

In a magic box, the words read the same across and down, just like this:

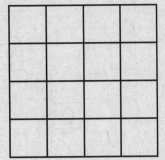

S	P	E	D
P	U	M	A
E	M	I	T
D	A	T	A

Have a go at making three more magic boxes using the words listed below, making sure that the word **DATA** appears once in each box.

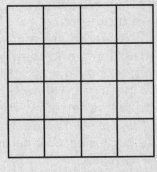

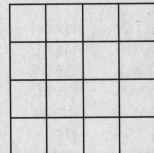

DATA	ORAL	ITEM
SODA	TENT	DATA
EDIT	ALAS	ANTS
TAME	DATA	AMEN

152 Add Up

The number in each circle is the total of the two below it. You can see that the white number must be 15 because 3 + 12 = 15. Can you work out all the numbers in the circles?

153 Trellis

Here's a kriss kross with a difference. All the words are four letters long, and they read diagonally downward to the right and to the left. The last letter of one word is the first of the next, and the circles show where the words start.

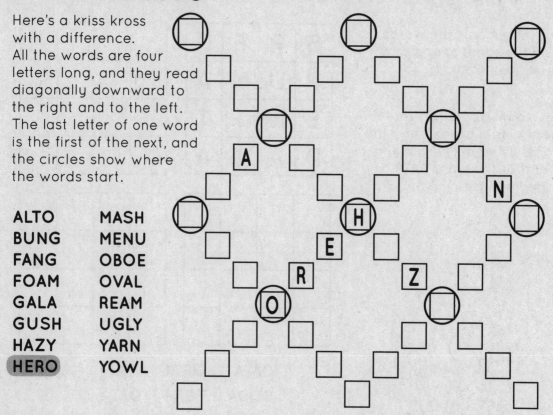

ALTO
BUNG
FANG
FOAM
GALA
GUSH
HAZY
HERO

MASH
MENU
OBOE
OVAL
REAM
UGLY
YARN
YOWL

154 Name Game

Complete the answers to these clues, then take the missing letters, in order, to spell out a type of breakfast cereal.

1 Bird of prey — FAL _ _ N
2 Person taking driving lessons — LEA _ _ ER
3 Perplex, stump — BAF _ _ E
4 Bread producer — B _ _ ER
5 Board game — CH _ _ S

155 Square Eyes

Two squares in this scene are identical, though they may not be the same way up. Which are they?

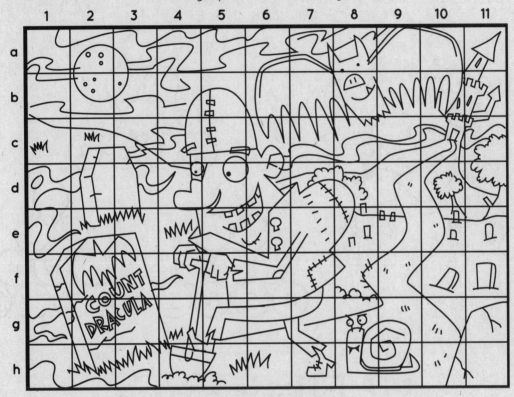

156 Spot the Sum

In each of these boxes, there are two numbers that can be added together to make one of the other numbers. For example, 2, 3, and 5 in a box would be the correct numbers because 2 + 3 = 5. Circle the correct three numbers in each box.

13   7   24   2   17   43   28   32   16

5   29   23   11   37   41   14   21   39

157 Pyramids

The number in each circle is the sum of the two below it, so in the first puzzle, the number shown in the third row down must be 3 because 2 + 1 = 3. Can you fill in all three pyramids?

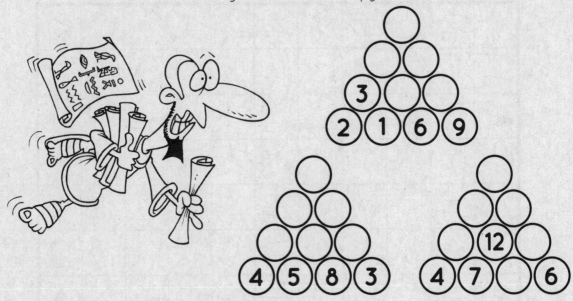

158 Elimination

Look at the categories, and cross out all the words that belong to any of those categories. You can start by crossing out all the FLOWERS in the list. When you've crossed out the words from all four categories, there will be two words left. Put these words together, and what do you get?

CATEGORIES
Fast foods • Types of bread • Toys • Things you get in the mail

Brown	Hot	PlayStation	Invitation
Burger	Doll	Postcard	Pogo stick
Yo-yo	Letter	Rye	Whole wheat
Parcel	Granary	Dog	Bills
Pizza	Kebab	Fries	White

159 Sudoku

Place numbers in the empty squares so that each row, each column, and each 2x2 block contains all the numbers from 1–4.

3	4	1	2
1	3	2	4

3		4	1
4			3
	3	1	

1			
	2		1
3		2	
			3

160 Rhyming Rows

Work out the answers to the clues and write them in the spaces provided. In each row, the answers rhyme. However, in each group of three, there is only one letter that appears in all three answers. If you write this letter in the box to the right of the grid, you will discover on which side a chicken has most feathers.

1 Become bigger (4)   2 Weeding tool (3)   3 Cut grass (3)

4 Not me (3)   5 Sticking paste (4)   6 Crossword hint (4)

7 Day, month, and year (4)   8 Four times two (5)   9 Hang around (4)

10 Goes by plane (5)   11 Purchases (4)   12 Weeps (5)

13 Sound of sadness (4)   14 Make a knot (3)   15 Pastry dish (3)

16 Naked, bare (4)   17 Impolite (4)   18 Things to eat (4)

19 Notice, look (3)   20 Bloodsucking insect (4)   21 Honey insect (3)

1		2		3		
4		5		6		
7		8		9		
10	FLIES	11	BUYS	12	CRIES	S
13		14		15		
16		17		18		
19		20		21		

161 Out of Order

Can you put the fourteen pictures below in order from the tallest chimney to the shortest?

162 Quest

All the answers to the clues are four-letter words. Enter them into the grid, starting from the outer squares. When you have done that, the innermost squares clockwise from number 9 will spell out something funny.

1 A film with a huge cast
2 Sport played on horseback
3 Not fat
4 Three times three
5 Repair
6 ___ Moore, actress
7 Brainwave
8 Piece of metal money

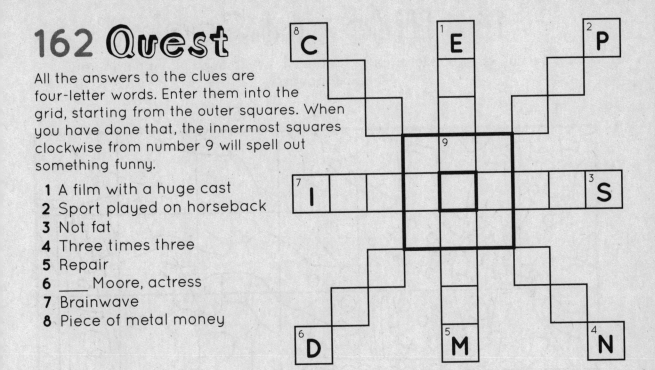

163 Cross Out

Each of the squares in this grid contains two letters. Can you cross out one letter in each square so that the remaining letters spell out words in all rows and columns? We've crossed out the **W** in the top left-hand square to start you off.

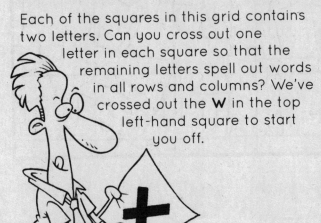

164 Hide and Seek

How quickly can you identify the squares in which each of the numbered shapes appears?

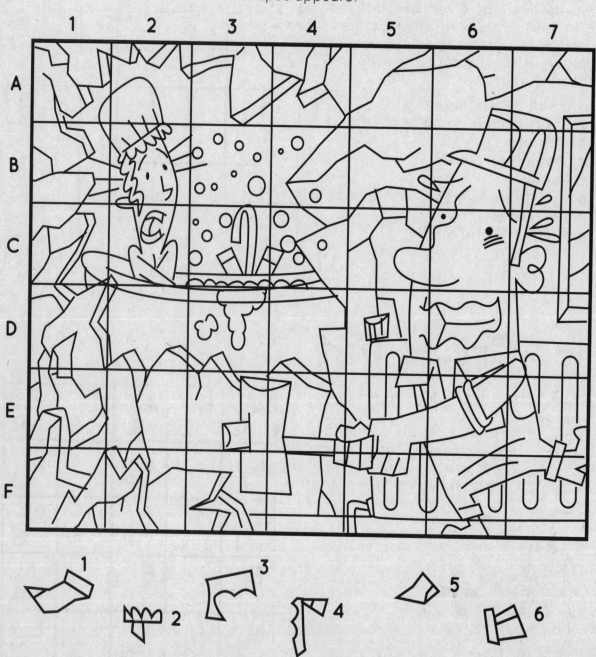

165 Egg Timer

To answer these clues, you have to remove a letter from the previous answer and (if necessary) rearrange the letters to get the new answer. When you pass clue 5, you have to do the opposite—add a letter each time. We have put in one answer to help you.

1 Mate, pal
2 Demon, ghoul
3 Discover, locate
4 Part of a fish
5 ~~___ you drop a glass it might break~~
6 Fruit with lots of seeds
7 Present
8 Argument
9 Journey by air

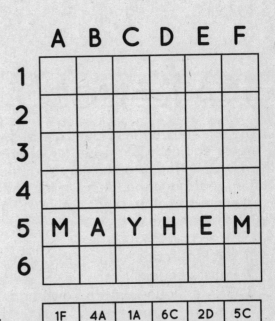

166 Splitz

The six-letter answers to these clues have been split into two in the jumbled heap of words below. Can you solve the clues by putting the words back together? When the grid is complete, transfer the letters to the appropriate boxes in the lower grid to reveal what smart piece of clothing a porker might wear.

1 Horse's fast pace
2 Wished for
3 Dry-roasted snack
4 Container for writing fluid
5 ~~Chaos, havoc~~
6 ____ down, on its head

TED   WAN   ~~MAY~~   POT   IDE   NUT

INK   PEA   UPS   ~~HEM~~   LOP   GAL

	A	B	C	D	E	F
1						
2						
3						
4						
5	M	A	Y	H	E	M
6						

1F	4A	1A	6C	2D	5C

167 Figurework

Have a go at fitting all the listed numbers into the grid.

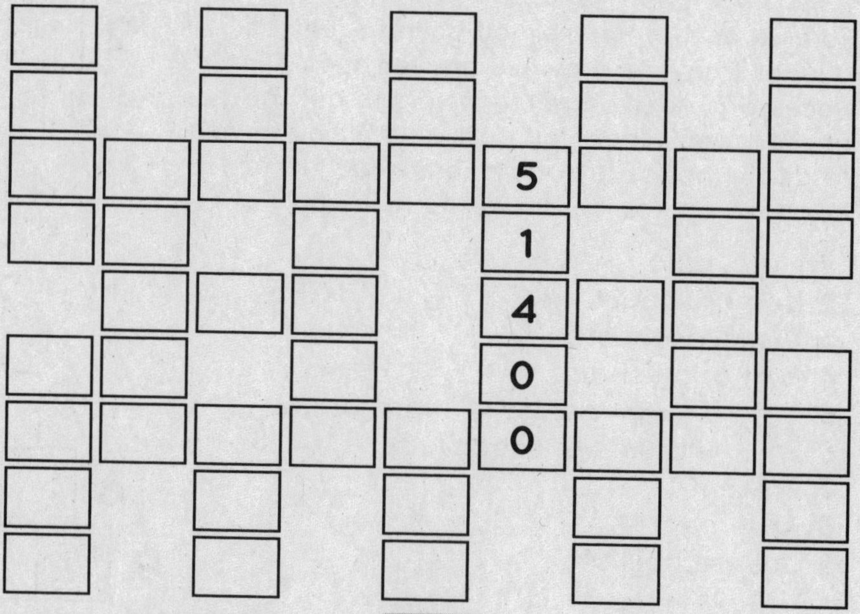

2 figures
32
46
58
85

3 figures
147
219
283
430
498
645
784
993

4 figures
1873
2866
5030
5995

5 figures
24882
32288
51400
74315

9 figures
730795426
981560920

168 X-word

The answers to these clues are all five-letter words ending in **S**, the center letter. Write your answers in the grid starting from the outer squares, then rearrange the letters in the shaded squares to spell out something that can go all around the world, yet stays in one corner.

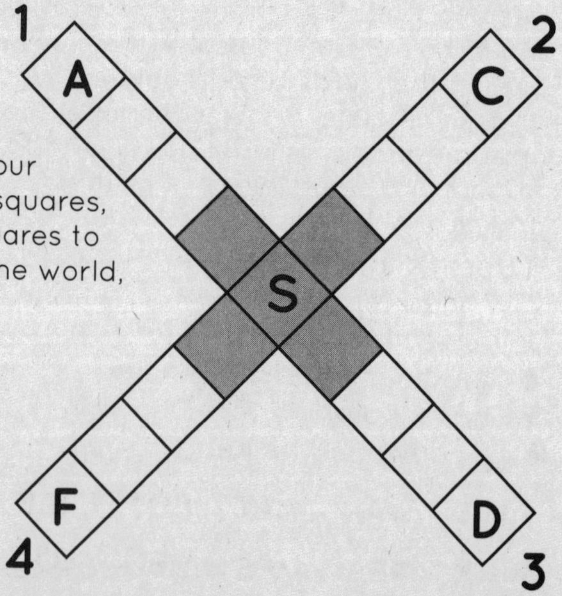

1 Book of maps
2 Potato snacks
3 Game played with arrows and a round board
4 Places with cows, sheep, horses, etc.

176 Where Am I?

If you can reconstruct this picture so that the left-hand side fits with the right-hand side, you will find out where this happy chap has been on vacation.

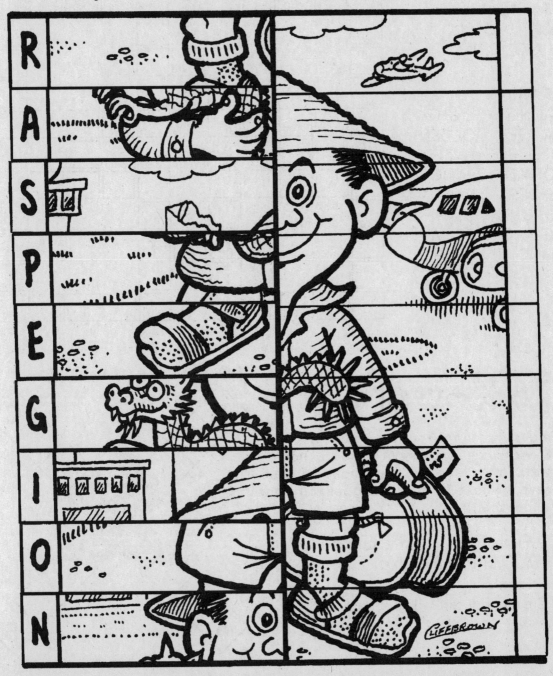

177 Gridwork

Can you fit all the listed words into the symmetrical grid below?

3 letters
CAT   OWL
DOG   ZOO

5 letters
ALLEY   LIGHT
ANGEL   OLDEN
DOZEN   PAGED
DRAIN   PATIO
EIDER   SALAD
FROWN   STAFF
GIANT   TOWER
GNOME   YACHT

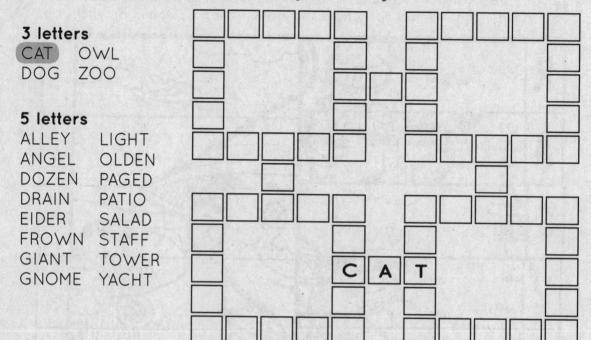

C A T

178 X-word

The answers to the four clues all end in **E**. Write your answers in the grid, then rearrange the letters in the shaded squares to reveal what sort of animal goes to bed with its shoes on.

1 Mickey ____, cartoon character
2 Long, narrow boat
3 Frighten
4 Clean yourself with water

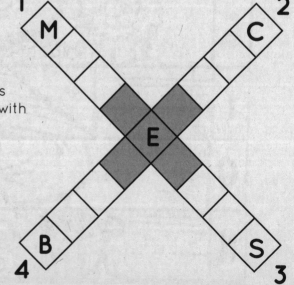

179 Quest

All the answers to the clues are four-letter words. Enter them into the grid, starting from the outer squares. When you have done that, the innermost letters clockwise from number 9 will spell out a part of the body.

1 Snake's noise
2 Money
3 Ring above an angel's head
4 List of meals
5 Tablet
6 Difficult, tough
7 Facial feature
8 Antlered animal

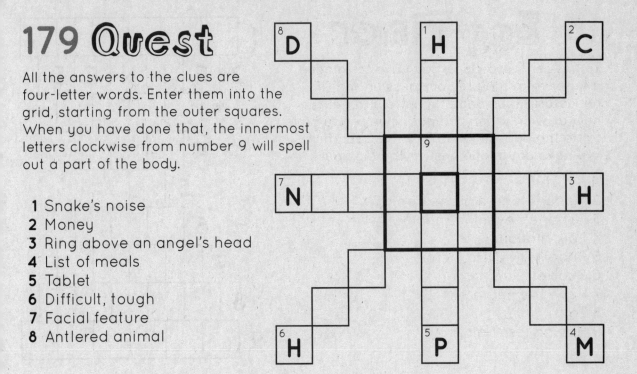

180 Cross Out

Each of the squares in this crossword grid contains two letters. Can you cross out one letter in each square, so that the remaining letters spell out words in all rows and columns? We've crossed out the W in the top left-hand square to start you off.

181 Egg Timer

To answer these clues, you have to remove a letter from the previous answer and (if necessary) rearrange the letters to get the new answer. When you pass clue 5, you have to do the opposite—add a letter each time. We have put in one answer to help you.

1 Pal, mate
2 ~~Made to pay a money penalty~~
3 Eat one's evening meal
4 Lair, hideout
5 Robert ____ Niro, actor
6 Scarlet
7 Have the nerve
8 Loaf
9 Having less hair

182 Splitz

The six-letter answers to these clues have been split into two in the jumbled heap of words below. Can you solve the clues by putting the words back together? When the grid is complete, transfer the letters to the appropriate boxes in the lower grid to reveal a musical insect.

1 Did not remember
2 Set of clothes
3 One who uses a bow and arrows
4 Boggy, swampy
5 ~~Dusk, twilight~~
6 Decorative drinking vessel

FIT   SHY   ~~GOB~~   ARC   SET   HER
SUN   MAR   OUT   ~~LET~~   GOT   FOR

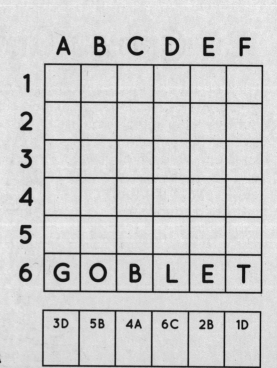

169 Change-a-letter

Solve the clues below, changing one letter of your answer at a time. When you get to clue 12, you'll find that its answer is also one letter different from the first answer, **BALE**.

1 Bundle of straw
2 Cook in the oven
3 Big pond
4 Frilly fabric
5 Be short of
6 Good fortune
7 Dirt
8 ___ Jagger, singer with the Rolling Stones
9 White drink
10 Measurement of distance
11 Man
12 Bargain event

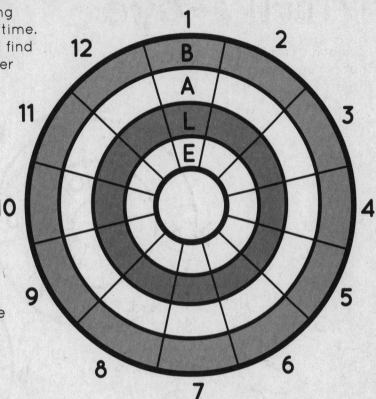

170 Sudoku

Place numbers in the empty squares so that each row, each column, and each 3x3 block contains all the numbers from 1–9.

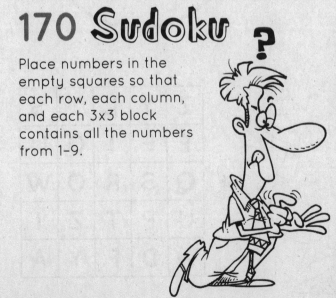

1	5	7		2	6			
		3						
6				4	1	8	5	
	1			5		2		
		1		5		2		3
9	3						2	5
2				9		6		7
		8	6	4	1			2
						9		
				2	9	3	4	6

171 Bull's-eye

For each of the targets, find two letters that, when placed in the center, will form three six-letter words.

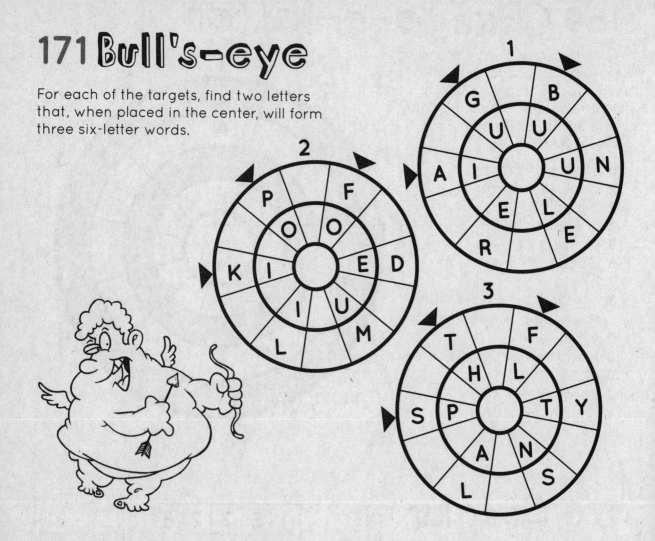

172 Break Out

Another animal has escaped from the zoo. If you cross out all the letters that appear more than once in the grid, the remaining letters will spell out what type of animal it is.

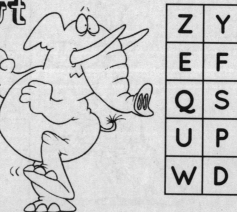

Z	Y	L	T	S
E	F	I	Q	U
Q	S	R	O	W
U	P	T	Z	I
W	D	F	Y	A

173 Alphabet Soup

To find out where Tim has been on vacation, work out which letters of the alphabet are missing from the scene and arrange them into a five-letter destination. And to discover where Mary will be spending her vacation, you'll need to rearrange the letters that appear three times.

I HAD A BRILLIANT TIME IN ○○○○○

I CAN'T WAIT TO GO TO ○○○○○

174 Trellis

Here's a kriss kross with a difference. All the words are four letters long, and they read diagonally downward to the right and to the left. The last letter of one word is the first of the next, and the circles show where the words start.

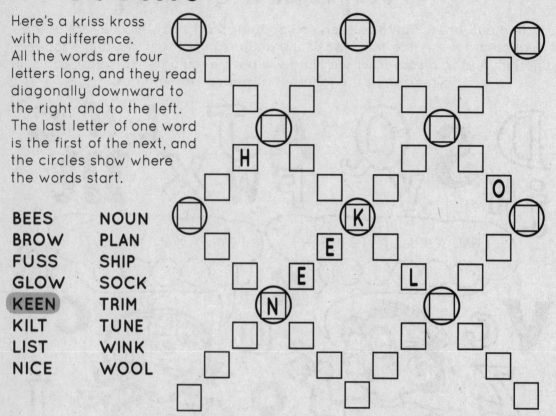

BEES   NOUN
BROW   PLAN
FUSS   SHIP
GLOW   SOCK
KEEN   TRIM
KILT   TUNE
LIST   WINK
NICE   WOOL

175 Name Game

Complete the answers to the clues, then take the missing letters in order to spell out something handy.

1 Instructor at school   T E A _ _ E R
2 Game in which you jump from square to square   H _ _ S C O T C H
3 Something to patch a wall   P L A _ _ E R
4 Two-wheeled transport   B _ _ Y C L E
5 Bag carried on your back   R U C _ _ A C K

186 Copy Cats

Can you pair up each lettered section with a numbered section to complete the twelve cats?

187 Gridwork

Can you fit all the listed words into the symmetrical grid?

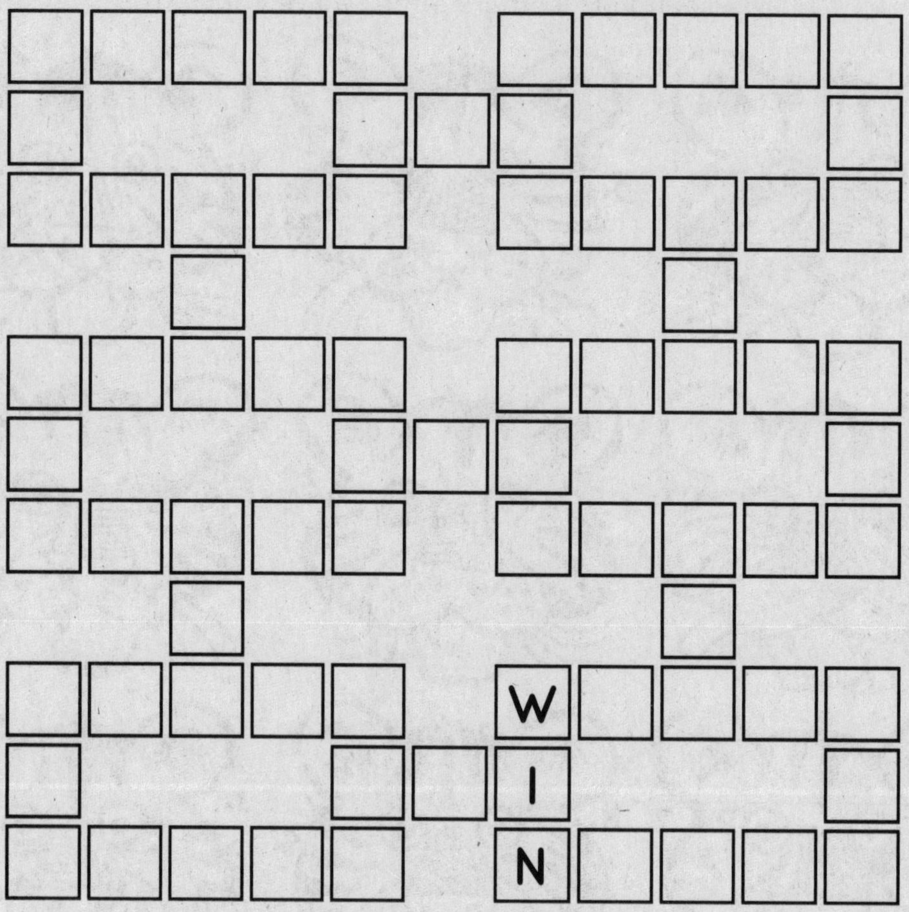

			W
			I
			N

3 letters
ALL
ASH
BAG
COD
DAB
EBB
HER
ICE

KEY
LEO
LOT
MAR
NOD
OAK
SKI
SKY
TOP

WIN
YAM

5 letters
BANAL
DOGMA
HYDRA
MEDAL
NASTY

PRISM
REACH
ROBOT
SONIC
TABBY
WHELK
YIELD

188 Pick-Me-Up

Can you decide in what order you would pick up the seven
eyedroppers if you could only take the top one each time?

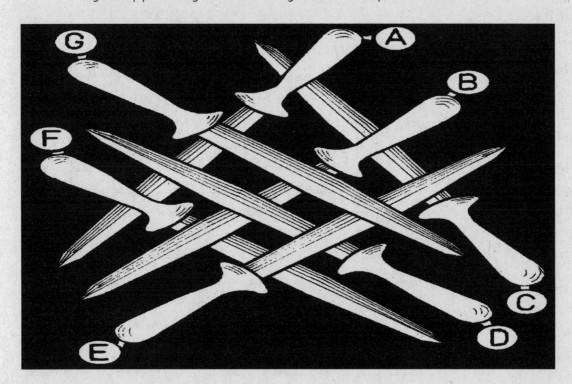

189 Matchblocks

Can you put each block from group A in front of a different block from group B
to make eight four-letter words? For instance, TH and EM can be put together to
form THEM. Now, see if you can match up the rest. Watch out, though—although
some group A blocks can match up with more than one block from group B, there
is only one way of using up all the blocks.

Group A

| TH | DI | KI | BO | HO | SU | SH | TW |

Group B

| EM | OF | IG | RF | SH | IP | NG | IL |

A	B		A	B		A	B
TH	EM						

190 Building Blocks

This kriss kross is all about buildings you might see in a town or city.

3 letters
PUB

4 letters
BANK
MILL
RINK

5 letters
BATHS
DEPOT
KIOSK
STORE

6 letters
ARCADE
CHURCH
GARAGE
MUSEUM
SCHOOL
TEMPLE

7 letters
COLLEGE
FACTORY
LIBRARY

8 letters
BOOKSHOP
LAWCOURT
TOWN HALL

9 letters
GYMNASIUM
JOB CENTER

10 letters
CHAIN STORE
DISTILLERY
NEWSAGENTS
POST OFFICE
RESTAURANT

11 letters
ANTIQUE SHOP
BEAUTY SALON

12 letters
TRAVEL AGENCY

NEWSAGENTS

191 Trellis

Here's a kriss kross with a difference. All the words are four letters long, and they read diagonally downward to the right and to the left. The last letter of one word is the first of the next, and the circles show where the words start.

BIAS
BLOT
COOT
HALO
HILL
INCH
LOSS
NEAP

NIGH
PLUM
POLO
SPAN
STAY
TAXI
TOWN
YELP

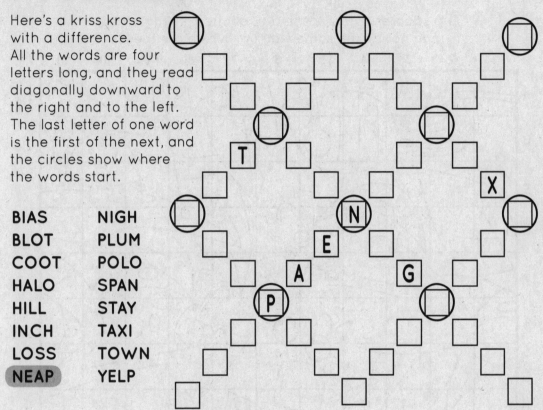

192 Name Game

Complete the answers to the clues, then take the missing letters, in order, to discover a type of rye bread.

1 Thing with a keyboard, monitor, mouse, etc. C O M _ _ T E R
2 The rabbit in *Bambi* T H U _ _ E R
3 ___ wheel, device that guides a car S T E _ _ I N G
4 Pay, salary E A R _ _ N G S
5 Farmyard bird C H I _ _ E N
6 Athlete's spear J A V _ _ I N

193 Square Eyes

Two squares in this scene are identical, though they
may not be the same way up. Which are they?

194 Spot the Sum

In each of these boxes, there are two numbers that can be
added together to make one of the other numbers. For example,
2, 3, and 5 in a box would be the correct numbers because
2 + 3 = 5. Circle the correct three numbers in each box.

11	9	8	12
16	15	22	5

4	12	11	14
9	24	22	1

195 Bull's-eye

For each of the targets, find two letters that, when placed in the center, will form three six-letter words.

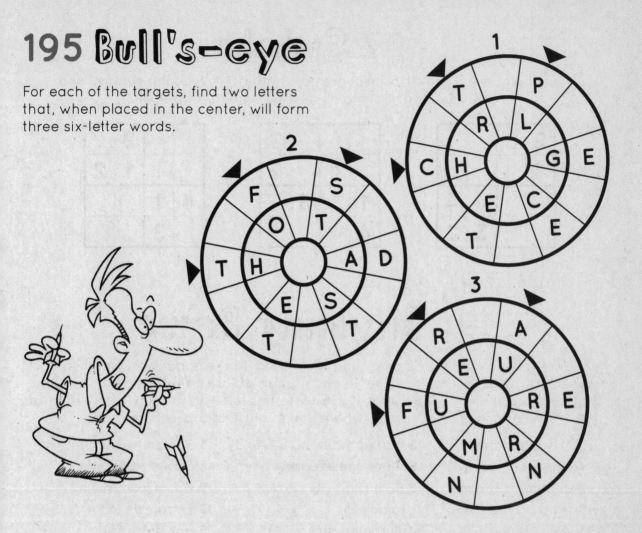

196 Break Out

Another animal has escaped from the zoo. If you cross out every letter in the grid that appears more than once and rearrange the remaining letters, you'll find out what type of animal is on the loose.

Q	T	U	E	I	P
J	N	G	R	K	L
F	L	W	S	V	A
H	R	P	O	J	V
T	A	Y	U	W	H
D	S	I	G	Q	F

197 Sudoku

Place numbers in the empty squares so that each row, each column, and each 2x2 block contains all the numbers from 1–4.

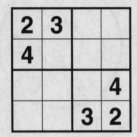

Grid 1:
2	3		
4			
		4	
		3	2

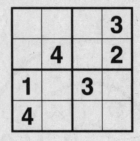

Grid 2:
			3
	4		2
1		3	
4			

Grid 3:
		3	
		1	2
4	1		
	3		

198 Rhyming Rows

Work out the answers to the clues and write them in the spaces provided. In each row, the answers rhyme. However, in each group of three, there is only one letter that appears in all three answers. If you write this letter in the box to the right of the grid, you will discover where you might find a prehistoric cow.

1 Arrive, reach (4) **2** Sound made by bees (3) **3** Beaten instrument (4)
4 Leak out, seep (4) **5** Opposite of win (4) **6** Doves' calls (4)
7 Uncooked bread (5) **8** Foot digit (3) **9** Cut a lawn (3)
10 Stop briefly (5) **11** Talons (5) **12** Entrances (5)
13 Lock opener (3) **14** Jumping insect (4) **15** Hot drink (3)
16 Line of people (5) **17** Look before ___ leap (3) **18** Sticky paste (4)
19 Exercise hall (3) **20** Rather dark (3) **21** That man (3)

1		2		3		
4	OOZE	5	LOSE	6	COOS	O
7		8		9		
10		11		12		
13		14		15		
16		17		18		
19		20		21		

199 Out of Order

Have a go at putting the pictures below in order, so that you start with the shortest-nosed swordfish and end with the longest.

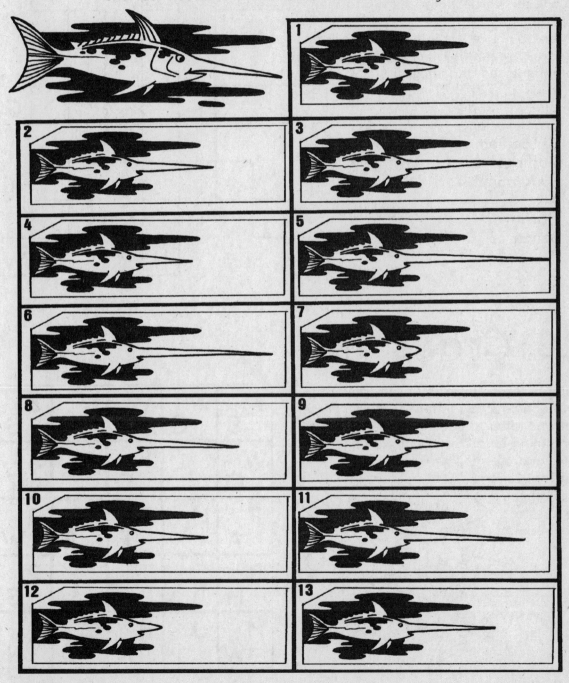

200 Quest

All the answers to the clues are four-letter words. Enter them into the grid, starting from the outer squares. When you have done that, the innermost squares around the number 9 will spell out something red and juicy.

1 Sidewalk edge
2 Small rodents
3 Garden entrance
4 Compass point opposite east
5 Sixty minutes
6 Nil
7 Martial art
8 Bench

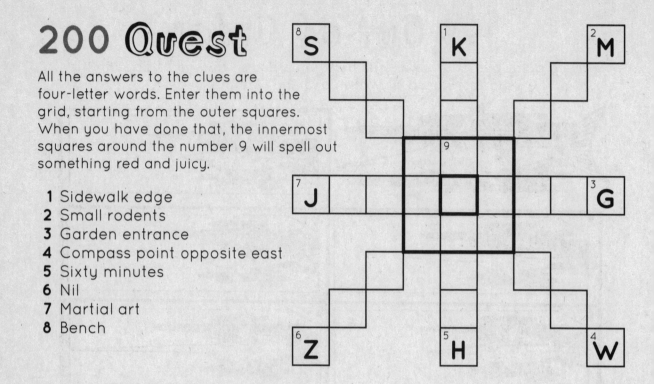

201 Cross Out

Each of the squares in this crossword grid contains two letters. Can you cross out one letter in each square so that the remaining letters spell out words in all rows and columns? We've crossed out the **K** in the top left-hand square to start you off.

202 Pirate Puzzle

Avast there, shipmates! We've got some famous pirates here for you to identify. Follow each one's trail to discover their name.

203 Figurework

Have a go at fitting all the listed numbers into the grid.

2 figures
12   51
24   62
35   89
47   90

5 figures
22441
32615
63458
70579

3 figures
160   544
280   621
325   792
448   889
453   918
517   966

7 figures
3105381
8613992

9 figures
156943927
239120840

6 3 4 5 8

204 X-word

The answers to the four clues all end in **T**. Write your answers in the grid, then rearrange the letters in the shaded squares to reveal what sort of coat has no buttons.

1 Burst out like a volcano
2 Rest on the surface of water
3 Huge horrible ogre
4 Boundary, outer edge

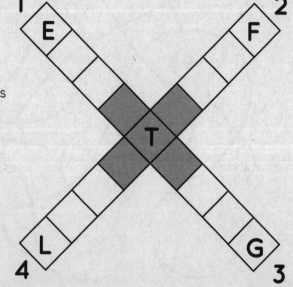

205 Change-a-letter

Solve the clues below, changing one letter of your answer at a time. When you get to clue 12, you'll find that its answer is also one letter different from the first answer, **FAKE**.

1 ~~Not genuine~~
2 Roast in the oven
3 Two-wheeled transport
4 Be fond of
5 Green citrus fruit
6 Hobble
7 Bedside light
8 Slightly wet
9 Live in a tent
10 Arrived
11 Identical
12 Stardom, celebrity

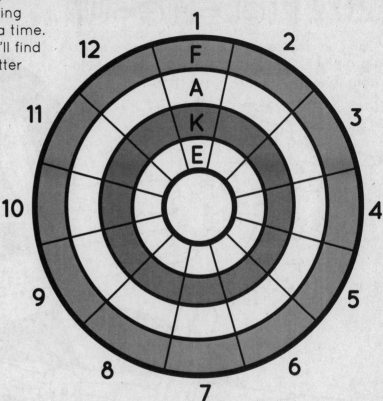

206 Sudoku

Place numbers in the empty squares so that each row, each column, and each 3x3 block contains all the numbers from 1–9.

2	9			5	8			
	7				9	2		
	4	5	3			7	6	
	8				3	6		
7	6						2	3
		2	6				9	
	2	3			1	9	5	
	7	5					3	
		2	3				1	7

207 Pick-Me-Up

Can you decide in what order you would pick up these twelve popsicle sticks if you could only take the top one each time?

208 Gridwork

Can you fit all the listed words into the symmetrical grid?

3 letters
AGE
AIM
COT
DOH
EEL
ELK
INN
LAG
MUD
OLD
ORB
OWN
PER
RIB
RUN
SOW
SUP
TOM
USE

4 letters
ABLE
AMID
BRIM
DEEP
EACH
INTO
MUSK
NUMB
ODDS
RENT
SNAP
WEIR

209 Add Up

The number in each circle is the total of the two below it. You can see that the white number must be 9 because 4 + 5 = 9. Can you work out all the numbers in the circles?

210 Alphabet Soup

To find out what this girl is called, work out which four letters of the alphabet are missing. When you have found all four, rearrange them to discover her name. The letters that appear three times will reveal what she's going to give her dog.

211 Smile Please

This puzzle is all about cameras and when we take pictures. Can you fit all the listed words into the grid?

4 letters
LENS
POSE
ZOOM

5 letters
FLASH
FOCUS
LIGHT
SHOOT
SMILE
SPOOL

6 letters
CAMERA
TRIPOD

7 letters
COMPOSE
HOLIDAY
SHUTTER
WEDDING

8 letters
BIRTHDAY
EXPOSURE
SNAPSHOT

10 letters
GRADUATION
VIEWFINDER

11 letters
CHRISTENING

C
A
M
E
R
A

212 Girls' Names

This puzzle is all about girls' names. See if you can find them all in this mini word search.

AMY

ANGELA

ANNE

LORNA

PAULINE

SUE

```
P Y A D W A S
R A V N N I U
U H U G R K E
F G E L S O E
A L N U I N L
A O N L R N Y
M J A H P M E
K B Z F A C B
E T L J Q P X
```

213 Magic Boxes

In a magic box, the words read the same across and down, just like this:

Have a go at making three more magic boxes using the words listed below, making sure that the word **NONE** appears once in each box.

P	I	N	T
I	V	O	R
N	O	N	E
T	R	E	E

NONE	ENDS	PEST
ANTS	NONE	OPEN
THIN	SNAP	HERO
NONE	NEED	IRON

214 Joking Apart

Have a go at matching each joke to its correct punchline.

1 What makes a chess player happy?
2 How do you keep cool at a soccer match?
3 What do you call an egg that enjoys playing tricks?
4 Why is history like a fruit cake?
5 What sits in the garden and calls his friends?
6 Who looks after a haunted beach?

A A practical yolker
B Because it's full of dates
C The ghost guard
D Taking the knight off
E A telegnome
F Sit next to a fan

215 Trellis

Here's a kriss kross with a difference. All the words are four letters long, and they read diagonally downward to the right and to the left. The last letter of one word is the first of the next, and the circles show where the words start.

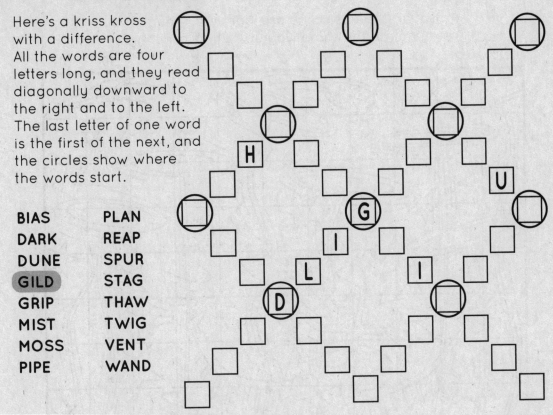

BIAS   PLAN
DARK   REAP
DUNE   SPUR
GILD   STAG
GRIP   THAW
MIST   TWIG
MOSS   VENT
PIPE   WAND

216 Name Game

Complete the answers to the clues, then take the missing letters in order to spell out what has patches without any stitches.

1 Get away   E S _ _ P E

2 Thief   R O _ _ E R

3 Hunting dog   B E _ _ L E

4 Truck fuel   D I _ _ E L

217 Square Eyes

Two squares in this scene are identical, though they
may not be the same way up. Which are they?

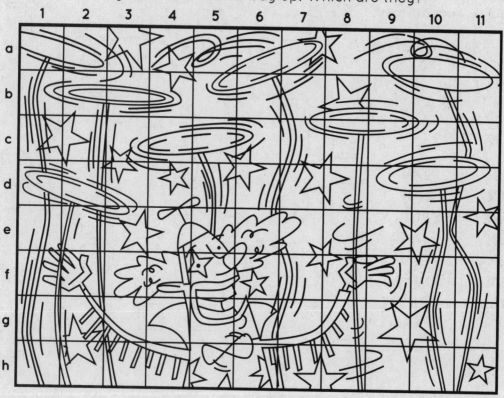

218 Spot the Sum

In each of these boxes, there are two numbers that can be added together
to make one of the other numbers. For example, 2, 3, and 5 in a box
would be the correct numbers because 2 + 3 = 5. Circle the correct three
numbers in each box.

22 31 44 5 19
11 7 23 34

26 9 32 2
4
21 37 18 12

219 Bull's-eye

For each of the targets, find two letters that, when placed in the center, will form three six-letter words.

220 Break Out

This man's pet has escaped. If you cross out every letter in the grid that appears more than once and rearrange the remaining letters, you'll find out what type of animal is on the loose.

N	B	V	C	A	D
D	F	H	O	J	K
L	S	X	G	Z	P
K	P	C	V	U	L
H	Z	E	A	N	F
M	P	B	G	J	X

221 Sudoku

Place numbers in the empty squares so that each row, each column, and each 3x3 block contains all the numbers from 1-9.

	1	5	7					3
9			4	1				5
7	8	6			5		4	
						1	7	
5				7				4
	3	7						
	5		3			8	2	9
8				5	6			7
3					1	4	5	

222 Cross Out

Each of the squares in this crossword grid contains two letters. Can you cross out one letter in each square so that the remaining letters spell out words in all rows and columns? We've crossed out the **B** in the top left-hand square to start you off.

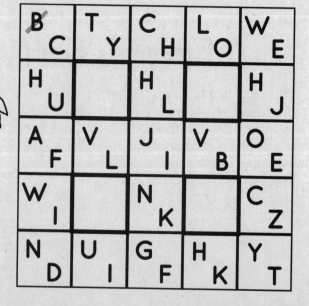

B C	T Y	C H	L O	W E
H U		H L		H J
A F	V L	J I	V B	O E
W I		N K		C Z
N D	U I	G F	H K	Y T

223 Out of Order

Have a go at putting these pictures in order, starting with the one showing the shortest tail and finishing with the longest.

224 Hide and Seek

How quickly can you identify the squares in which
each of the numbered shapes appears?

225 Egg Timer

To answer these clues, you have to remove a letter from the previous answer and (if necessary) rearrange the letters to get the new answer. When you pass clue 5, you have to do the opposite—add a letter each time. We have put in one answer to help you.

1 Title given to a male adult
2 Minute parasites
3 ~~The hour of the day~~
4 To fasten with cord or string
5 That thing
6 To be seated
7 A place where a building, town, etc., is
8 The rise and fall of the oceans
9 Walk purposefully

226 Splitz

The six-letter answers to these clues have been split into two in the jumbled heap of words below. Can you solve the clues by putting the words back together? When the grid is complete, transfer the letters to the appropriate boxes in the lower grid to discover an alloy of tin and lead.

1 Young cat
2 Baby's woolen footwear
3 Traffic ____, person who gives out parking fines
4 Young farm animal
5 ~~Sad film that might make you cry~~
6 Male parent

TEN   HER   ~~WEE~~   BOO   FAT   TEE
DEN   KIT   LET   ~~PIE~~   PIG   WAR

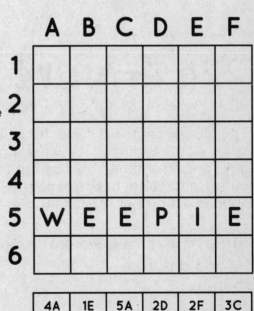

227 Figurework

Have a go at fitting all the listed numbers into the grid.

2 figures
27
33
81
94

3 figures
171
239
321
457
490
543
624
736
785
970

4 figures
1001
2010

5 figures
15430
22546
62034
87170

7 figures
5361724
9800137

9 figures
241385103
367799488
704901163
917406128

228 X-word

The answers to these clues are all five-letter words ending in the letter **Y**. Write your answers in the grid starting from the outer squares, then rearrange the letters in the shaded squares to spell out a boy's name.

1 Race involving several runners and a baton
2 Tale
3 Striped cat
4 Tired

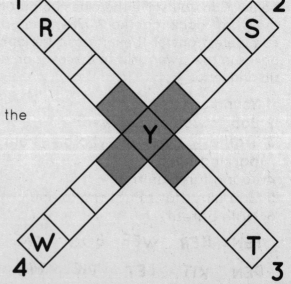

229 Who Does What?

Follow the trails from each of these kids and you'll find out what they want to be when they grow up.

230 Alphabet Soup

Work out which five letters of the alphabet are missing and then rearrange them to reveal the violinist's name.

231 Out of Order

Can you put the eighteen pictures below in order, starting with the unshaded yacht and ending with the one that is completely darkened?

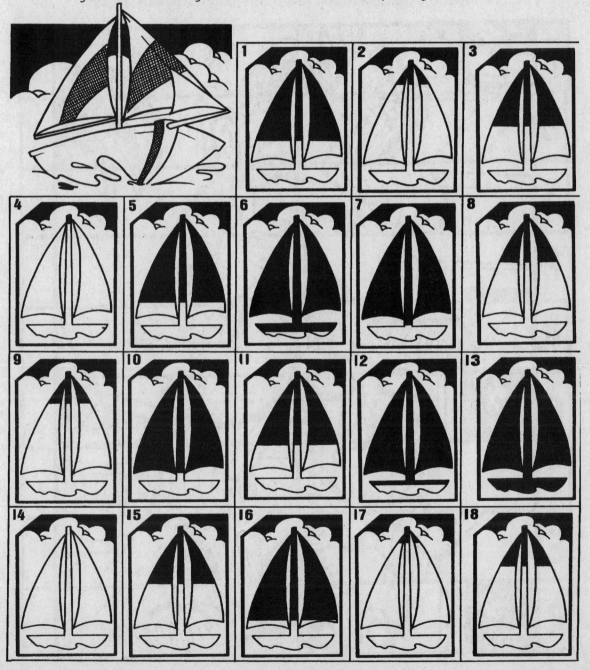

232 What's My Line?

If you can reconstruct this picture correctly, the letters reading
down the left-hand side will reveal the character's profession.

Solutions

1 QUEST
1 Sent 2 Poor 3 Taxi 4 Puma 5 Mean
6 Wing 7 Gill 8 Kite: **TRIANGLE**

2 CROSS OUT

```
C H A I R
R   L   A
E X A C T
A   R   T
M U M M Y
```

3 EGG TIMER
1 Garden 2 Grand 3 Darn 4 Ran 5 An
6 Man 7 Mane 8 Named 9 Demand

4 SPLITZ
1 Garage 2 Eyelid 3 Cotton
4 Bowman 5 Window 6 Action:
WOMBAT

5 FIGUREWORK

```
9 5 0 3     7 7 4 3
2 9   3 4 8   8 1
1 7 7   0   4 9 0
9   4 2 2 9 6   0
      1 9 9
4   6 4 7 6 5   2
2 7 5   6   8 6 5
1 3   5 1 3   9 2
5 6 4 4   6 3 0 8
```

6 X-WORD
1 Paris 2 Boots 3 Wings 4 Beans:
STING

7 CHANGE-A-LETTER
1 Ring 2 Wing 3 Wine 4 Pine 5 Pile
6 Pale 7 Pane 8 Pang 9 Bang
10 Band 11 Rand 12 Rind

8 TAKE FIVE
1 Boots 2 Fence 3 Snake 4 Lunch
5 Month: **BEACH**

9 BULL'S-EYE
1 US 2 CI 3 AU

10 LEFTOVERS
BUS

11 GRIDWORK

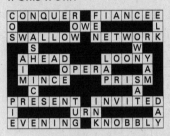

```
C O N Q U E R   F I A N C E E
O           O W E           L
S W A L L O W   N E T W O R K
    S           W           Y
    A H E A D   L O O N Y
    I     O P E R A         A
    M I N C E     P R I S M
    C                       A
P R E S E N T   I N V I T E D
I           U R N           A
E V E N I N G   K N O B B L Y
```

12 CLOCKWORDS
1 Race 2 Wins 3 Laps 4 Time 5 Pace
6 Lane 7 Pass 8 Ties

13 WORD LADDER
1 Slap 2 Slip 3 Ship 4 Shop

14 MAGIC BOXES

```
S H E D    H E R D    M E S H
H E R O    E V E N    E L L E
E R O S    R E N T    S L U R
D O S E    O N T O    H E R O
```

15 DOUBLE TROUBLE
1 Boys, slow
2 Taxi, iron
3 Ball, lamb
4 Goal, love
5 Easy, year.
The adjective in the gray circles
is **SILLY** and the one in the gray
squares is **BRAVE**!

16 TRELLIS

```
  H         P             A
  A     E     A       F
  I E     I A     A
      L     R I
      E A     O I S
  S     S     T     K
  S O         W O I
  O N         W L
    G           N
    L   O E A V
  O     A S V
W           T       Y
```

17 NAME GAME
1 Entrance 2 Grandmother
3 Hospital 4 Starts 5 Center
6 Wetsuit: **TRANSPARENTS**

18 SQUARE EYES
Squares A8 and D4.

19 SPOT THE SUM
1 12 + 17 = 29 2 3 + 18 = 21

20 PYRAMIDS

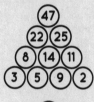

```
        47
      22  25
     8  14  11
    3  5  9  2
```

```
        29
      12  17
     7  5  12
    6  1  4  8
```

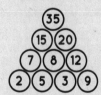

```
        35
      15  20
     7  8  12
    2  5  3  9
```

21 ELIMINATION
GIRLS' NAMES: Helen, Jane, Mary,
Susan, Catherine.

FAMILY MEMBERS: aunty, brother,
father, mother, uncle.

STAR SIGNS: Aries, Capricorn,
Libra, Scorpio.

HATS: beret, cap, sombrero, turban.

The two leftover words are **PHONE**
and **MOBILE**, which make **MOBILE
PHONE**

22 SUDOKU

1	4	2	3
3	2	1	4
4	1	3	2
2	3	4	1

2	1	3	4
4	3	2	1
1	2	4	3
3	4	1	2

2	4	1	3
3	1	4	2
1	3	2	4
4	2	3	1

23 RHYMING ROWS

1 Paw 2 Explore 3 Poor
4 Lie 5 Goodbye 6 Eye
7 Rein 8 Pain 9 Lane
10 Pie 11 Pry 12 Ply
13 Maze 14 Rays 15 Laze
16 Sleigh 17 Play 18 Lay
19 Saw 20 Score 21 Snore:
PEN-PALS

24 SHADOW PLAY

9, 3, 14, 2, 7, 12, 5, 1, 10, 4, 11, 6, 13, 8

25 QUEST

1 Cash 2 Judo 3 Beam 4 Tree
5 Flew 6 Echo 7 Year 8 Beak:
HOMEWORK

26 CROSS OUT

S	A	V	E	R
L		I		A
E	N	D	E	D
E		E		I
P	H	O	T	O

27 EGG TIMER

1 Mother 2 Homer 3 Home 4 Hoe
5 He 6 Her 7 Hare 8 Heart
9 Father

28 SPLITZ

1 Pantry 2 Settee 3 Mayhem
4 Zipper 5 Maggot 6 Father:
NAZRAT

29 FIGUREWORK

30 X-WORD

1 Texas 2 Lambs 3 Tiles
4 Lions: **BEANS**

31 CHANGE-A-LETTER

1 Bank 2 Bunk 3 Buck 4 Duck
5 Dunk 6 Sunk 7 Sink 8 Wink
9 Wind 10 Wand 11 Sand 12 Band

32 SUDOKU

1	5	6	8	2	4	7	9	3
9	7	2	3	1	5	4	6	8
4	3	8	7	6	9	2	5	1
8	4	5	6	3	2	9	1	7
2	6	7	1	9	8	5	3	4
3	9	1	5	4	7	6	8	2
6	2	4	9	8	1	3	7	5
7	8	9	4	5	3	1	2	6
5	1	3	2	7	6	8	4	9

33 BULL'S-EYE

1 GG 2 RP 3 RT

34 LEFTOVERS

SOLID

35 GRIDWORK

C	A	M	E	O		A	C	O	R	N		S	H	A	R	K
O			D	I	P			E	L	K						I
B	I	P	E	D		T	E	M	P	O		I	N	G	O	T
								I								
T	H	R	O	B		V	I	X	E	N		F	L	U	S	H
I			E	R	A			O	U	R						A
P	R	O	N	G		N	A	M	E	D		Y	E	A	R	S

BONUS — WHEELY WORDS

The center letter is **E** and the
numbers are: 1 Twenty 2 One
3 Eight 4 Twelve 5 Hundred
6 Three

36 ALPHABET SOUP

The girl's name is **MARY** and her
horse is called **DUKE**

37 CLOCKWORDS

1 Gift 2 Cake 3 Star 4 Dove 5 Card
6 List 7 Give 8 Post

38 BREAK OUT

The missing instrument is a **FLUTE**

39 MAGIC BOXES

T	R	A	P
R	A	C	E
A	C	H	E
P	E	E	L

D	A	R	T
A	F	A	R
R	A	C	E
T	R	E	E

S	C	A	R
C	O	L	A
A	L	E	C
R	A	C	E

40 WORD LADDER

1 Ness 2 Nest 3 Test 4 Best
5 Beat

41 TRELLIS

42 NAME GAME

1 Palace 2 Present 3 Barbie
4 Salad 5 Ladder: **LASER BLADE**

43 SQUARE EYES

Squares B1 and F9.

44 SPOT THE SUM

1 9 + 17 = 27   2 8 + 19 = 27

45 PYRAMIDS

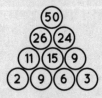

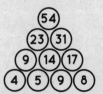

46 ELIMINATION
BOYS' NAMES: Peter, Michael, John, George, Tim.

MONTHS: January, March, November, April, December.

SPORTS: football, golf, basketball, hockey.

PARTS OF THE BODY: leg, arm, elbow, knee.

The two leftover words are **WINKS** and **FORTY**, which make **FORTY WINKS**

47 SUDOKU

4	1	2	3
3	2	4	1
1	4	3	2
2	3	1	4

4	1	2	3
3	2	1	4
1	4	3	2
2	3	4	1

4	2	1	3
1	3	2	4
3	1	4	2
2	4	3	1

48 RHYMING ROWS
1 Boo 2 Blue 3 Blew
4 High 5 Lie 6 Pie
7 Saw 8 Sore 9 Score
10 Toe 11 Row 12 Mow
13 Corn 14 Pawn 15 Fawn:
BISON

49 OUT OF ORDER
3, 10, 16, 11, 5, 19, 1, 8, 17, 7, 12, 15, 2, 18, 6, 4, 14, 13, 9

50 QUEST
1 Wife 2 Roar 3 Bare 4 Grow
5 Zero 6 Meal 7 Calf 8 Crew:
WEREWOLF

51 CROSS OUT

52 EGG TIMER
1 Health 2 Heath 3 Heat 4 Eat 5 ET
6 Net 7 Rent 8 Enter 9 Center

53 SPLITZ
1 Repeat 2 Settee 3 Canyon
4 Rotten 5 Copper 6 Nitwit:
PANTRY

54 FIGUREWORK

55 X-WORD
1 Rings 2 Venus 3 Yours 4 Atlas:
SUGAR

56 CHANGE-A-LETTER
1 Pang 2 Gang 3 Sang 4 Sank
5 Tank 6 Task 7 Mask 8 Mash
9 Cash 10 Cast 11 Past 12 Pant

57 SUDOKU

3	1	7	4	8	2	5	6	9
2	8	6	9	3	5	4	1	7
5	9	4	1	7	6	2	8	3
1	7	2	3	6	9	8	4	5
4	5	3	8	1	7	6	9	2
9	6	8	2	5	4	7	3	1
7	2	9	6	4	1	3	5	8
6	3	1	5	2	8	9	7	4
8	4	5	7	9	3	1	2	6

58 BULL'S-EYE
1 PE 2 BB 3 SE

59 BREAK OUT
LIZARD

60 ALPHABET SOUP
The man's name is **LUKE**, and he's an **ACTOR**

61 CLOCKWORDS
1 Tree 2 Bush 3 Park 4 Barn
5 Farm

62 SIX DOWN
1 Shop 2 Four 3 Knee 4 Page
5 Frog 6 Keys. The word is
HUNGRY

63 MAGIC BOXES

S	H	I	P
H	I	D	E
I	D	E	A
P	E	A	R

A	S	K	S
S	H	I	P
K	I	L	O
S	P	O	T

M	A	S	K
A	C	H	E
S	H	I	P
K	E	P	T

64 LETTER PYRAMID
1 So 2 Los 3 Also 4 Salon
The fish is **SALMON**

65 TRELLIS

66 NAME GAME
1 Passage 2 Cuckoo 3 Heroine:
SAUCER

67 SQUARE EYES
Squares B5 and E2.

68 SPOT THE SUM
1 9 + 26 = 35 2 11 + 28 = 39

69 PYRAMIDS

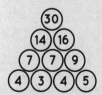

70 ELIMINATION

BABY: bush, cry, jelly, test-tube, war.

CHURCH: aisle, alter, apse, font, nave.

FLOWERS: crocus, hyacinth, iris, rose, tulip.

PIANO: grand, key, stool, tuner, upright.

The two leftover words are **BOLT** and **THUNDER**, which make **THUNDERBOLT**

71 SUDOKU

4	2	3	1
3	1	4	2
1	4	2	3
2	3	1	4

3	1	4	2
4	2	1	3
1	3	2	4
2	4	3	1

2	1	3	4
3	4	2	1
4	2	1	3
1	3	4	2

72 RHYMING ROWS

1 Igloo 2 Grew 3 Glue
4 Crow 5 Ago 6 Foe
7 Knee 8 Ski 9 Key
10 Bass 11 Case 12 Face
13 Err 14 Purr 15 Stir
16 Eight 17 Crate 18 Wait:
GO-KART

73 OUT OF ORDER

2, 9, 18, 7, 1, 13, 6, 16, 8, 14, 4, 10, 17, 5, 15, 12, 3, 11

74 QUEST

1 Pens 2 Talc 3 Zero 4 Yo-yo 5 Last
6 Five 7 Star 8 Owls: **SCOOTERS**

75 CROSS OUT

76 HIDE AND SEEK

1 A1 2 C2 3 A6 4 C5 5 F6 6 F7

77 EGG TIMER

1 Recipe 2 Price 3 Ripe 4 Pie 5 PE
6 Pea 7 Cape 8 Place 9 Plaice

78 SPLITZ

1 Donkey 2 Bootee 3 Punnet
4 Nutmeg 5 Magpie 6 Tarmac:
BARNEY

79 FIGUREWORK

80 X-WORD

1 Erupt 2 Split 3 Bleat 4 Pilot:
PATIO

81 CHANGE-A-LETTER

1 Wide 2 Wade 3 Wave 4 Wake
5 Bake 6 Cake 7 Case 8 Cash
9 Mash 10 Wash 11 Wish 12 Wise

82 SUDOKU

3	1	9	2	6	8	4	5	7
8	4	5	7	1	9	6	2	3
2	7	6	3	5	4	9	1	8
7	9	8	1	2	5	3	4	6
4	3	2	6	8	7	1	9	5
6	5	1	9	4	3	7	8	2
9	8	7	4	3	2	5	6	1
1	2	3	5	9	6	8	7	4
5	6	4	8	7	1	2	3	9

83 BULL'S-EYE

1 CH 2 AG 3 VE

84 BREAK OUT

SANDWICH

85 ALPHABET SOUP

Jim is going to **TURKEY** and Sarah is going to **SPAIN**

86 TRELLIS

87 NAME GAME

1 Tomato 2 Batter 3 Stereo
4 School 5 Hornet: **MATTERHORN**

88 QUEST

1 Boss 2 Jump 3 Lane 4 Dove
5 Hand 6 Thaw 7 Flea 8 Gray:
SPEEDWAY

89 CROSS OUT

R	I	G	H	T
A		L	O	
D	R	I	N	K
I		D	E	
O	C	E	A	N

90 EGG TIMER

1 Daring 2 Drain 3 Rain 4 Ran 5 An
6 Can 7 Clan 8 Lance 9 Cleans

91 SPLITZ

1 Sunhat 2 Button 3 Barrow
4 Tomcat 5 Goodie 6 Fibbed:
HUMBUG

92 FIGUREWORK

93 X-WORD

1 Spire 2 Stone 3 Grape
4 Venue: **PRUNE**

94 CHANGE-A-LETTER
1 Dart 2 Bart 3 Bark 4 Park 5 Pack
6 Pick 7 Kick 8 Mick 9 Mice 10 Dice
11 Dire 12 Dirt

95 LOSE THE LETTERS
The word is **SOAKED**

96 BULL'S-EYE
1 IE 2 BU 3 AY

97 LEFTOVERS
HENS

98 GRIDWORK

99 PICK-ME-UP
2, 5, 3, 8, 7, 6, 12, 10, 11, 9, 1, 4

100 MATCHBLOCKS
Mule, soap, leaf, bill, face, bark,
food, plop

101 MAGIC BOXES

S	O	A	P
O	N	C	E
A	C	T	S
P	E	S	T

A	S	K	S
S	O	A	P
K	A	T	E
S	P	E	D

V	A	S	T
A	H	O	Y
S	O	A	P
T	Y	P	E

102 BREAK OUT
The animal is a **DONKEY**

103 TRELLIS

104 NAME GAME
1 Passage 2 Cuckoo 3 Heroine:
SAUCER

105 SQUARE EYES
Squares B10 and C4.

106 SPOT THE SUM
1 9 + 27 = 36 2 8 + 23 = 31

107 PYRAMIDS
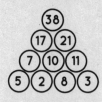

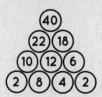

108 ELIMINATION
FRUIT: banana, apple, orange,
strawberry, pear.

VEGETABLES: onion, potato,
carrot, lettuce, cucumber.

KITCHEN UTENSILS: spoon, fork,
knife, spatula.

BIG CATS: lion, tiger, puma,
cheetah.

The two leftover words are
PROCESSOR and **FOOD**, which
make **FOOD PROCESSOR**

109 SUDOKU

2	1	3	4
4	3	2	1
1	2	4	3
3	4	1	2

2	3	1	4
1	4	2	3
4	2	3	1
3	1	4	2

3	4	1	2
1	2	3	4
2	3	4	1
4	1	2	3

110 RHYMING ROWS
1 Days 2 Sleighs 3 Raise
4 Cue 5 Blue 6 Gnu
7 Shone 8 John 9 Swan
10 Shy 11 High 12 Sigh
13 Axe 14 Wax 15 Packs
16 Motto 17 Lotto 18 Gateau:
SUNHAT

111 OUT OF ORDER
17, 5, 15, 7, 2, 18, 4, 14, 1, 16, 3, 10, 11,
6, 12, 8, 13, 9

112 QUEST
1 Toss 2 Term 3 Menu 4 Long
5 Slug 6 Heel 7 Gale 8 Bear:
SMUGGLER

113 CROSS OUT

114 EGG TIMER
1 Island 2 Snail 3 Nail 4 Ian 5 In
6 Pin 7 Pint 8 Paint 9 Taping

115 SPLITZ
1 Ashore 2 Carpet 3 Supper
4 Pantry 5 Gadget 6 Punnet:
CHERRY

116 FIGUREWORK

117 X-WORD
1 Sighs 2 Slugs 3 Quits 4 Adios:
GHOST

118 CHANGE-A-LETTER
1 Feel 2 Fuel 3 Full 4 Bull 5 Ball
6 Hall 7 Hill 8 Pill 9 Till 10 Tall 11 Tell
12 Fell

119 SUDOKU

8	9	7	1	3	2	6	4	5
2	4	3	9	5	6	8	1	7
5	6	1	4	8	7	2	9	3
1	5	6	8	2	9	3	7	4
4	2	8	5	7	3	9	6	1
3	7	9	6	4	1	5	8	2
9	8	4	2	1	5	7	3	6
6	3	2	7	9	4	1	5	8
7	1	5	3	6	8	4	2	9

120 BULL'S-EYE

1 LL **2** ME **3** AD

121 LEFTOVERS

CROW

122 GRIDWORK

123 ADD UP

```
        96
      60  36
    38  22  14
  22  16  6   8
```

124 ALPHABET SOUP

The man's name is **HENRY** and he's eating **OXTAIL** soup

125 IT'S ALL OVER

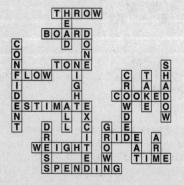

126 MIXED FRUITS

127 MAGIC BOXES

O	V	E	R
V	I	L	E
E	L	S	E
R	E	E	F

D	E	A	R
E	L	S	E
A	S	P	S
R	E	S	T

E	L	S	E
L	O	O	P
S	O	M	E
E	P	E	E

128 JOKING APART

1 D **2** F **3** A **4** B **5** E **6** C

129 TRELLIS

130 NAME GAME

1 Swallow **2** Garden **3** Tomorrow
4 Liberty: **WARDROBE**

131 SQUARE EYES

Squares C5 and D11.

132 SPOT THE SUM

1 14 + 17 = 31 **2** 9 + 28 = 37

133 PYRAMIDS

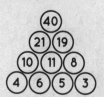

134 ELIMINATION

SIMPSONS CHARACTERS: Homer, Marge, Bart, Lisa, Maggie.

MUSICAL INSTRUMENTS: piano, guitar, trumpet, drum.

FISH: herring, salmon, cod, pike.

DRINKS: water, milk, juice, tea, coffee.

The two leftover words are **SWIMMING** and **POOL**, which make **SWIMMING POOL**

135 SUDOKU

3	1	4	2
2	4	1	3
1	2	3	4
4	3	2	1

1	3	4	2
2	4	3	1
3	2	1	4
4	1	2	3

3	4	1	2
2	1	3	4
4	3	2	1
1	2	4	3

136 RHYMING ROWS

1 Key **2** Knee **3** Ski
4 John **5** Gone **6** Swan
7 Picks **8** Six **9** Fix
10 Glue **11** Through **12** Grew
13 Shy **14** Thigh **15** High
16 True **17** Two **18** Stew: **KNIGHT**

137 OUT OF ORDER

11, 1, 18, 9, 3, 16, 6, 14, 5, 17, 2, 13, 7, 15, 8, 4, 12, 10

138 QUEST
1 Twig 2 Echo 3 Lava 4 Pull 5 Help
6 Judo 7 Kiss 8 Moat: **GOALPOST**

139 CROSS OUT

M	A	G	I	C
O		U		O
D	R	E	A	M
E	■	S	■	I
M	U	S	I	C

140 EGG TIMER
1 Ladder 2 Dread 3 Dare 4 Red
5 ER 6 Her 7 Hero 8 Shore
9 Horses

141 SPLITZ
1 Window 2 Repair 3 Hamper
4 Madden 5 Geneva 6 Refuse:
NEPHEW

142 FIGUREWORK

143 X-WORD
1 Brake 2 House 3 Algae 4 White:
SKATE

144 CHANGE-A-LETTER
1 Foal 2 Coal 3 Coat 4 Boat 5 Boot
6 Root 7 Hoot 8 Hook 9 Book
10 Cook 11 Cool 12 Fool

145 SUDOKU

1	4	2	7	9	8	3	5	6
6	8	7	3	5	1	2	9	4
3	5	9	6	2	4	1	8	7
8	9	6	4	3	5	7	1	2
2	1	3	9	8	7	6	4	5
5	7	4	2	1	6	8	3	9
9	3	8	5	7	2	4	6	1
4	2	5	1	6	3	9	7	8
7	6	1	8	4	9	5	2	3

146 BULL'S-EYE
1 VI 2 OO 3 NG

147 BREAK OUT
ZEBRA

148 ALPHABET SOUP
The girl's name is **JUDY** and
the kitten's name is **FELIX**

149 TUNE IN

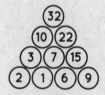

150 AT THE BEACH

151 MAGIC BOXES

D	A	T	A
A	M	E	N
T	E	N	T
A	N	T	S

S	O	D	A
O	R	A	L
D	A	T	A
A	L	A	S

E	D	I	T
D	A	T	A
I	T	E	M
T	A	M	E

152 ADD UP
```
      93
    43  50
  15  28  22
 3  12  16  6
```

153 TRELLIS

154 NAME GAME
1 Falcon 2 Learner 3 Baffle
4 Baker 5 Chess: **CORNFLAKES**

155 SQUARE EYES
Squares B5 and E9.

156 SPOT THE SUM
1 7 + 17 = 24 **2** 14 + 23 = 37

157 PYRAMIDS

158 ELIMINATION
FAST FOODS: burger, pizza, fries,
kebab.

TYPES OF BREAD: brown, granary,
rye, wholemeal, white.

TOYS: yo-yo, doll, PlayStation,
pogo stick.

THINGS YOU GET IN THE POST:
Parcel, letter, postcard, invitation,
bills.

The two leftover words are **HOT**
and **DOG**, which make **HOT DOG**

159 SUDOKU

3	4	1	2
2	1	4	3
4	2	3	1
1	3	2	4

3	2	4	1
4	1	2	3
1	4	3	2
2	3	1	4

1	3	4	2
4	2	3	1
3	1	2	4
2	4	1	3

160 RHYMING ROWS
1 Grow **2** Hoe **3** Mow
4 You **5** Glue **6** Clue
7 Date **8** Eight **9** Wait
10 Flies **11** Buys **12** Cries
13 Sigh **14** Tie **15** Pie
16 Nude **17** Rude **18** Food
19 See **20** Flea **21** Bee: **OUTSIDE**

161 OUT OF ORDER
9, 13, 3, 11, 2, 8, 14, 1, 7, 10, 4, 12, 6, 5

162 QUEST
1 Epic **2** Polo **3** Slim **4** Nine **5** Mend
6 Demi **7** Idea **8** Coin: **COMEDIAN**

163 CROSS OUT

164 HIDE AND SEEK
1 A4 **2** B2 **3** C7 **4** C4 **5** D1 **6** E5

165 EGG TIMER
1 Friend **2** Fiend **3** Find **4** Fin **5** If
6 Fig **7** Gift **8** Fight **9** Flight

166 SPLITZ
1 Gallop **2** Wanted **3** Peanut
4 Inkpot **5** Mayhem **6** Upside:
PIGSTY

167 FIGUREWORK

168 X-WORD
1 Atlas **2** Chips **3** Darts **4** Farms:
STAMP

169 CHANGE-A-LETTER
1 Bale **2** Bake **3** Lake **4** Lace **5** Lack
6 Luck **7** Muck **8** Mick **9** Milk **10** Mile
11 Male **12** Sale

170 SUDOKU
1	5	7	2	6	3	4	8	9
8	4	3	7	9	5	2	6	1
6	2	9	4	1	8	5	3	7
7	1	4	5	8	2	6	9	3
9	3	6	1	7	4	8	2	5
2	8	5	9	3	6	1	7	4
3	9	8	6	4	1	7	5	2
4	6	2	3	5	7	9	1	8
5	7	1	8	2	9	3	4	6

171 BULL'S-EYE
1 RG **2** SS **3** OR

172 BREAK OUT
LEOPARD

173 ALPHABET SOUP
Tim has been to **EGYPT** and
Mary is going to **CHINA**

174 TRELLIS

175 NAME GAME
1 Teacher **2** Hopscotch **3** Plaster
4 Bicycle **5** Rucksack: **CHOPSTICKS**

176 WHERE AM I?
He's been to **SINGAPORE**

177 GRIDWORK

178 X-WORD

1 Mouse **2** Canoe **3** Scare **4** Bathe:
HORSE

179 QUEST
1 Hiss **2** Cash **3** Halo **4** Menu **5** Pill
6 Hard **7** Nose **8** Deer: **SHOULDER**

180 CROSS OUT

181 EGG TIMER
1 Friend **2** Fined **3** Dine **4** Den **5** De
6 Red **7** Dare **8** Bread **9** Balder

182 SPLITZ
1 Forgot **2** Outfit **3** Archer **4** Marshy
5 Sunset **6** Goblet: **HUMBUG**

183 WHAT'S MY LINE
1 Electrician **2** Travel agent
3 Fishmonger

184 CHANGE-A-LETTER
1 Find **2** Bind **3** Band **4** Bend **5** Bond
6 Bone **7** Lone **8** Lane **9** Land
10 Sand **11** Wand **12** Wind

185 HIDDEN WORDS
1 Last ye**AR I ES**pecially wanted a
computer.
2 In **CAPRI CORN**flakes are eaten
every day.
3 The **GEM IN I**rene's pendant is
amethyst.
4 I hate brocco**LI, BRA**n and liver.
5 Pi**LE O**ranges in the glass fruit
bowl.
6 A slum**P IS CES**sation of
profitable trade.
7 The quiz contestant had to
choose either mollu**SC OR PIO**neer.

186 COPY CATS
A-9, **B**-8, **C**-7, **D**-6, **E**-10, **F**-11, **G**-12,
H-1, **I**-2, **J**-4, **K**-3, **L**-5

187 GRIDWORK

188 PICK-ME-UP
G, E, D, B, F, A, C

189 MATCHBLOCKS
THEM, DISH, KING, BOIL, HOOF, SURF, SHIP, TWIG

190 BUILDING BLOCKS

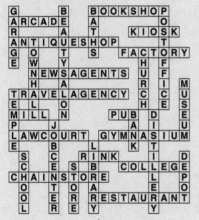

191 TRELLIS

192 NAME GAME
1 Computer 2 Thumper 3 Steering
4 Earnings 5 Chicken 6 Javelin:
PUMPERNICKEL

193 SQUARE EYES
Squares B1 and F4.

194 SPOT THE SUM
1 11 + 5 = 16   2 4 + 7 = 11

195 BULL'S-EYE
1 AN 2 RE 3 TU

196 BREAK OUT
DONKEY

197 SUDOKU

198 RHYMING ROWS
1 Come 2 Hum 3 Drum
4 Ooze 5 Lose 6 Coos
7 Dough 8 Toe 9 Mow
10 Pause 11 Claws 12 Doors
13 Key 14 Flea 15 Tea
16 Queue 17 You 18 Glue
19 Gym 20 Dim 21 Him: **MOOSEUM**

199 OUT OF ORDER
7, 12, 1, 9, 4, 10, 2, 13, 8, 3, 11, 6, 5

200 QUEST
1 Kerb 2 Mice 3 Gate 4 West 5 Hour
6 Zero 7 Judo 8 Seat: **BEETROOT**

201 CROSS OUT

S	C	R	U	B
W		O		A
A	M	B	E	R
R		I		G
M	I	N	C	E

202 PIRATE PUZZLE
1 Henry Morgan
2 Anne Bonny
3 John Avery

203 FIGUREWORK

	2		1		
4	4	8	3	2	5
3	5		6	2	1	4	7
2	3	9	1	2	0	8	4	0
6		6	3	4	5	8		5
1	5	6	9	4	3	9	2	7
5	1		9	1	8		8	9
	7	9	2		1	6	0	
	0		2	

204 X-WORD
1 Erupt 2 Float 3 Giant 4 Limit: A
coat of **PAINT**

205 CHANGE-A-LETTER
1 Fake 2 Bake 3 Bike 4 Like 5 Lime
6 Limp 7 Lamp 8 Damp 9 Camp
10 Came 11 Same 12 Fame

206 SUDOKU

2	9	6	7	5	8	3	4	1
3	7	1	4	6	9	2	8	5
8	4	5	3	1	2	7	6	9
5	8	9	1	2	3	6	7	4
7	6	4	9	8	5	1	2	3
1	3	2	6	4	7	5	9	8
4	2	3	8	7	1	9	5	6
6	1	7	5	9	4	8	3	2
9	5	8	2	3	6	4	1	7

207 PICK-ME-UP
4, 1, 5, 2, 3, 6, 8, 10, 12, 7, 9, 11

208 GRIDWORK

209 ADD UP
```
      29
    15  14
   9   6   8
  4   5   1   7
```

210 ALPHABET SOUP
The girl's name is **JUDY** and she's
going to give her dog a **BATH**

211 SMILE PLEASE

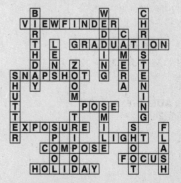

212 GIRLS' NAMES

213 MAGIC BOXES

T	H	I	N
H	E	R	O
I	R	O	N
N	O	N	E

S	N	A	P
N	O	N	E
A	N	T	S
P	E	S	T

N	O	N	E
O	P	E	N
N	E	E	D
E	N	D	S

214 JOKING APART
1 D **2** F **3** A **4** B **5** E **6** C

215 TRELLIS

216 NAME GAME
1 Escape **2** Robber **3** Beagle
4 Diesel: **CABBAGES**

217 SQUARE EYES
Squares A8 and E9.

218 SPOT THE SUM
1 11 + 23 = 34 **2** 9 + 12 = 21

219 BULL'S-EYE
1 NG **2** MP **3** MB

220 BREAK OUT
MOUSE

221 SUDOKU

4	1	5	7	6	9	2	8	3
9	2	3	4	1	8	7	6	5
7	8	6	2	3	5	9	4	1
2	6	4	5	9	3	1	7	8
5	9	8	1	7	2	6	3	4
1	3	7	6	8	4	5	9	2
6	5	1	3	4	7	8	2	9
8	4	2	9	5	6	3	1	7
3	7	9	8	2	1	4	5	6

222 CROSS OUT

223 OUT OF ORDER
15, 6, 18, 1, 10, 21, 13, 4, 16, 8, 20, 3, 11,
19, 9, 17, 7, 12, 2, 14, 5

224 HIDE AND SEEK
1 C7 **2** B4 **3** A2 **4** A6 **5** F7 **6** E3

225 EGG TIMER
1 Mister **2** Mites **3** Time **4** Tie **5** It
6 Sit **7** Site **8** Tides **9** Stride

226 SPLITZ
1 Kitten **2** Bootee **3** Warden **4** Piglet
5 Weepie **6** Father: **PEWTER**

227 FIGUREWORK

	5	3	6	1	7	2	4	
		6	2	0	3	4		
9	1	7	4	0	6	1	2	8
4	5	7		1		3	2	1
		4	9	0		7	8	5
2	3	9		2		5	4	3
7	0	4	9	0	1	1	6	3
		8	7	1	7	0		
	9	8	0	0	1	3	7	

228 X-WORD
1 Relay **2** Story **3** Tabby **4** Weary:
BARRY

229 WHO DOES WHAT?
1 Woodwork teacher
2 A space traveler
3 A speech therapist

230 ALPHABET SOUP
The violinist's name is **BRUCE**

231 OUT OF ORDER
14, 4, 17, 2, 9, 18, 8, 15, 3, 11, 1, 5, 16,
10, 7, 12, 6, 13

232 WHAT'S MY LINE?
He's a Professor